FOLLOW THE GLEAM

A History of the Liberal
Religious Youth Movements

FOLLOW THE GLEAM

A History of the Liberal Religious Youth Movements

by Wayne B. Arnason

a Flaming Chalice monograph from

Skinner House   Boston   1980

For Jon T.

his five thousand indian motorcycles

and all the people who rode them with me

CONTENTS

PREFACE

This book began in 1973 as a personal research project for my own entertainment during a stifling and boring summer studying theological German at Harvard Divinity School. The Universalist Historical Library at Tufts was a cool and restful treasure house of fascinating information about a rich history behind our U-U youth movements that I had known little about.

This would have remained only a personal project if not for the encouragement and tireless support of Carl Seaburg. As he has done with many other authors in our movement, Carl suggested that everything about my project could be better than it was. He encouraged me to pursue publication of the manuscript by Skinner House, and did much of the fund-raising himself. The interlude memoirs between the chapters were his idea, and he patiently nudged me to find more and better pictures. Carl has also been a meticulous editor.

Follow the Gleam would not be in print without Carl Seaburg, and I owe him a deep debt of gratitude.

Many other members, past and present, of the Unitarian and Universalist youth groups have helped in the compiling of this history. Those whose personal support for me has been much appreciated are too numerous to mention. I would single out a few who have made specific contributions.

Alan Seaburg and Cate Hitchings have been very helpful in my research.

The Unitarian Sunday School Society has offered a generous grant towards this publication, as has the Continental Youth Adult Committee.

Eugene Navias, Starr Williams, Eugene Pickett, Robert Senghas, Robert West and Leon Hopper read early versions of the manuscript and offered valuable suggestions.

David Parke offered a most thorough critique on the manuscript and his fund-raising efforts on my behalf were magnificent.

Dr. Conrad Wright supervised my writing of the final draft of the manuscript during my last semester at Harvard. I wish the final result was more of a credit to his excellent help.

Many youth group veterans have been generous with their time in writing me memoirs, providing photographs, and answering my questions. Besides those whose memoirs have been printed and whose names are listed in the table of contents, I also wish to thank Dick Kuch, Alice Harrison, Dana Greeley, Dick Woodman, Peter Baldwin, Deither Gehrmann, Leon Hopper, Chuck Eddis, Chris Raible, Peter Raible, and Richard Kossow for their help.

The shortcomings and errors of interpretation or fact are, of course, my own responsibility. I only wish that more names, more stories, more details could have been offered, especially in the index of youth leaders in Appendix 1 and 2. There wasn't enough room and there wasn't enough time. I suppose there never is.

Wayne Arnason
April 28, 1980
Boston, MA

ii

ACKNOWLEDGMENTS

These individuals and organizations helped to make publication of this book possible. We are most grateful to them for their encouragment.

Continental Youth Adult Committee, UUA; Unitarian Sunday School Society

Donald Harrington; Walter Donald Kring

Clement and Margaret Bried, Nancy Doughty, James C. Lee, Wendy O'Donnell, John & Margaret Redston, Richard Taeuber.

Jane Anderson, John & Lilia Arnason, Charles Eddis, Leon Hopper, Edward J. Kingsbury, Richard Kuch, Robert H. MacPherson, Gordon & Phyllis McKeeman, David Parke, Christopher Raible, Peter Raible, Robert C. & Margie G. Sallies, Carl Seaburg, Benevolent Fraternity.

James Luther Adams, Peter A. Baldwin, Josiah Bartlett, George K. Beach, Wendy Coe, Jerry & Denise Davidoff, Stephen Fritchman, John Gibbons, John S. Gilbert, Joan Goodwin, Dana Greeley, Alice M. Harrison, James & Betty Hulse, William P. Jenkins, Lawrence Ladd, Ruth Luening, Gretchen Loomis Manker & Raymond George Manker, George Marshall, Alexander Meek, Jack Mendelsohn, Roberta King Mitchell, Tracy M. Pullman, Barbara E. Sakuma, Lillian Schayer, Peter Scott, Winchell & Helen Dally Smith, Mildred S. Vickers, Arnold Westwood, Liberal Religious Youth of Sacramento, CA; Unitarian Universalist Church Women's Alliance, Oak Ridge, TN.

Howard Box, Janet Bowering, George Brigham, Carol Morrill Brock & John Booth Brock, David Glickman, Susanne McNamara, D'Alton B. Myers, M. Melvina Svec; Sunnyvale, CA Unitarian Universalist Fellowship

iii

1

INTRODUCTION

A perennial problem within churches of all denominations is programming
for young people. Secular educators have a relatively easy task compared
to religious educators when they approach people in this awkward space
between childhood and adulthood. Secular educators move into more
specialized, complex, and advanced fields of study, giving greater
responsibility and freedom of choice to the students in determining the
direction of their own education. Religious educators must ask themselves
a far more difficult question: what are the religious needs and questions
of people at this stage of life, and how are they best met?

Since the turn of the century, the liberal religious churches of North
America have answered these questions in many different ways, befitting
the congregational system of polity under which we operate. However a
dominant model for the religious education of young adults over this
century has been that of the institutional youth group. Youth groups
are not considered as religious education classes per se. The adults who
work with them do not consider themselves teachers, but advisors. There is
usually no predetermined curriculum. The young people themselves participate
directly in determining a program for the group that will meet the needs and
questions that are apparent.

In addition, most youth groups organize themselves constitutionally in
one form or another. They seek to institutionalize the fact that they are
not a church school class any longer in the way that they have been before.
Their religious education has moved into a different phase, modelled on
the educational groups and institutions through which adult people seek
to continue their education and growth. In secular public education, the
only opportunity students have for a similar learning experience is in
the extra-curricular interest groups, such as the drama club or the student

government. Even then, this depends on the attitude taken by the teacher-advisor or the school administration.

Since the late nineteenth century when this model of religious education for youth became widespread, the youth groups of the Unitarian and Universalist churches in North America have maintained national and continental unions to serve their needs and represent their interests within the denominational structure. At first, these groups supported a continental structure on their own. Later, with the advent of the "United Appeal" style of fund-raising, the churches included them under their funding umbrella.

The young people of the Universalist Church banded together into The Young People's Christian Union (Y.P.C.U.) in 1889. The Unitarian young people created The Young People's Religious Union (Y.P.R.U.) in 1896. Both groups reorganized themselves in 1941, becoming respectively The Universalist Youth Fellowship (U.Y.F.) and American Unitarian Youth (A.U.Y.). In the year 1953 they voted to merge into one united youth organization, Liberal Religious Youth (L.R.Y.), anticipating the move towards federal union of the Unitarian and Universalist denominations.

My goal in writing a history of the institutional youth movement within the Unitarian Universalist Association and its predecessors is two-fold.

To begin with, I want to trace the growth and development of the movement over the past century for the benefit of the young people and adults who are currently involved or interested in our youth movement, embodied at this writing in Liberal Religious Youth. On the local level, L.R.Y. groups rise and fall with each succeeding generation of high school students. L.R.Y. advisors are only rarely involved for longer than a few years. Each new L.R.Y. Executive Committee member arrives in Boston to begin work with only the haziest notion of what has happened in years past. There are very few people who have any sense of the continuity of our youth movement.

There is continuity, however. Indeed, there are patterns that have remained fairly constant over the years. Most people are aware that many notable leaders within the Unitarian Universalist movement began their denominational involvement through the youth groups. John Haynes Holmes, Frederick May Eliot, Roger Etz, Dorothy Tilden Spoerl, Dana Greeley, Max Kapp, Gordon McKeeman, and the Raible family are some examples. One might anticipate upon seeing names like these that the relationships between the adult church and the youth groups were much better in the past than they have ever been in the present. This is not the case. There has always been a degree of ambivalence and tension between the churches and their youthful counterparts.

L.R.Y.'ers on the local and regional levels have often been critical of the continental level of L.R.Y. for its alienation from the grass roots, its inefficiency, and its extravagent spending habits.[1] This same complaint echoes all through the movement's history. Tensions and differences between the various structural levels of the movement have always existed. They reflect the same lack of commitment to a centralized institutional framework that characterizes the adult churches.[2]

The youth leaders of today grapple with the problem of how to be helpful and relevent to the people at the local level. Yet even when the youth organization was centered mainly in New England, the jump from regional to national or continental office has always represented a quantum leap in perspective and in problems for the people involved.

Finally, meeting the needs of college age people within the youth movement has always been a difficult and usually disappointing task.

I do not wish to point only to the continuities over the eighty-seven years of the youth movement's history. The second goal of my narrative is to indicate the changes as well. How did the L.R.Y. of today - a unique, continent-wide, youth organization incorporated, staffed, and governed exclusively by people from the ages of fourteen to nineteen - evolve out of a young people's movement brought into being by a small group of New England ministers near the turn of the century?

A dominant theme within our youth movement over the years is summarized in the slogan "youth autonomy". At first glance it appears that "youth autonomy" has been a guiding principle in our approach to youth programming right from the beginning. In the 1924 "Youth Issue" of The Universalist Leader, Stanley Manning, Director of Young People's Work within the Universalist Convention for four and one half years, wrote:

> The first joy to be found in such a position is the discovery
> that no one can be a director of young people's work. There
> is so much of initiative, of willingness to work, of desire to
> explore and discover on their part that no one can direct their
> activities...This does not mean that there is not entire will-
> ingness to discuss methods and ways of working, that there is
> no desire for advice and assistance; but the very genius of
> young people's work lies in its self-direction.[3]

Almost forty years later, in 1963, L.R.Y. President Maria Fleming wrote:

> L.R.Y. is not autonomous of adults; we depend on adults for
> their counsel in the functioning of our organizations; we need
> their experience and knowledge as we set up programs, conduct
> workshops, and write pamphlets; we depend on advisors to
> chaperone our functions so that we can hold these functions;
> we depend on the financial support of the denomination for
> the very existence of continental Liberal Religious Youth.
> And yet, we do have some meaning in mind when we talk about

youth autonomy now, we mean basically the right for youth
to determine their own programs. This means that we think
no one knows better what young people are interested in than
young people themselves. This is not to say that young people
can carry out all of their ideas most effectively however.
In youth-determined programs, young people decide what they
want and carry out these programs with the help and most
effective use of adults who have the background to help them.[4]

The ideas and ideals sound the same, but in actuality they have come
to mean very different things over the years. The phrase "youth autonomy"
was not widely used until after 1947, but in terms of real independence
the youth groups of the thirties were more autonomous than L.R.Y. has ever
been. Stanley Manning is describing the capability of young people to run
programs of their own. Fleming is arguing for a right to self-determination,
above and beyond the ability of youth to carry out programs entirely on
their own.

One reason for changes in the youth movement over the years has been
that the age of the participants has been dropping steadily ever since the
1920's, to the point where the L.R.Y. leaders of today are now rarely older
than eighteen. Each drop in the age level of the movement has moved it
into a new phase and a new self-understanding.

The expansion of the program from its New England base into a truly
continental one took over fifty years to accomplish, and that greatly
altered the character of the movement as well.

Finally, the merger into Liberal Religious Youth represented a
journey into uncharted waters. Many of the differences which would later
be argued out in the final Unitarian Universalist merger process were
encountered in the creation of L.R.Y. Liberal Religious Youth was an organ-

ization different from its predecessors in structure and style. The L.R.Y. of today is also different from what it has been before. Changes in culture create changes in institutions, and the history of youth movement must be examined in this light as well.

This narrative has inevitably become an institutional history of the liberal religious youth movement. The scope of the manuscript and the requirements of composing a comprehensive historical survey have meant that a great deal of what is at the heart of the movement is not reflected here. The personal memoirs between the chapters capture a little of the "heart" to which I am referring. What has made Y.P.C.U., Y.P.R.U., A.U.Y., U.Y.F., and finally L.R.Y. and S.R.L. so important has been the quality and depth of the interpersonal relationships that have been formed and grown within the context of these groups. The most important stories that the people who were in these groups would tell are probably not the ones that are told here. They would be stories of time spent together going through some of the significant rites of passage in human life. They would be personal stories of adventure, and friendship, and fear, and love. They would be stories of a process of religious education which is unique within the religious institutions of North America.

Chapter 1: LAYING THE FOUNDATIONS

The youth movements of the Universalist and Unitarian churches had their beginnings in a larger groundswell of "youth" activity across the denominational spectrum in the late nineteenth century. This was in turn one aspect of a more general movement of voluntary organizations within churches that produced women's groups, alter guilds, men's clubs, etc. Of course, both the Universalist and Unitarian churches had long-standing Sunday School societies, and Sunday School programs devised by denominational committees or local churches included material for those in "senior" grades (today's high school age).

However, there was no specific young people's organization on any national or continental level. It appears that already in American institutional religion the period between fourteen and thirty was distinguished as a "problem" time, an explosive time loaded with energy that needed to be channelled. Dwight L. Moody, the famous evangelist, perceived the potential of a student religious movement as early as 1866 when he organized the Student Volunteer Movement for Christian Missions.

The Unitarians and Universalists made no such specific efforts. Jenkin Lloyd Jones, the renowned Missionary Secretary of the Western Unitarian Conference, began what he called a Mutual Improvement Club in 1874 in his church in Janesville, Wisconsin. It was to be "a combination of post-graduate Sunday School study, adult education, and social service and reform work."[1]

The idea caught on in the Western Unitarian Conference. These groups began to be known as Unity Clubs. Their largely literary and philosophical programs were well attended by people under the age of thirty-five. By 1882 there were thirty such Unity Clubs. However, these were not "young people's groups" in the sense that we would use that term today. High school age people were not involved in them.[2]

The event which initiated the proliferation of church groups specifically intended for young people occured in 1881 in the Williston
Congregational Church in Portland, Maine. There the Reverend F.E. Clark
founded a Young People's Society for Christian Endeavor (Y.P.S.C.E.).
Clark's idea spread throughout Congregational churches and into other
denominations as well. Between 1881 and 1889 some thirty-eight Christian
Endeavor Societies were founded in Universalist Churches.

The Lynn Convention

The Universalist General Convention (U.G.C.) attempted as early as
1884 to organize these groups into a single Universalist youth organization.
In 1886 the U.G.C. Committee on Mission Boxes proposed a plan to create a
unified Young People's Missionary Society with branches in every church.
The response to the idea was not overwhelming. By 1889 fifty-five of
these Missionary Society groups had been brought into the fold or created,
but there were numerous Universalist young people's groups that remained
unaffiliated with any larger body.

The potential for a single youth movement was there however. Some
young ministers in western New York began in 1883 to publish a newspaper
for Universalist young people entitled The Universalist Union. Among the
publishers was the Reverend Stephen Herbert Roblin. Shortly afterwards
he took a church in Bay City, Michigan, and there organized a highly
successful Y.P.S.C.E. group.[3] He and two other members of the group, Albert
C. Grier and Alfred J. Cardell, were particularly interested in propagating
the idea of a national union. Together they initiated a letter to all
Universalist young people's societies calling for a national organization
of Universalist young people.

The response was mixed. Mr. Grier wrote in 1889:

There followed dark days. Replies poured in and at times I dreaded to open my mail. Discouragements of all sorts came upon us. But few had any such society. Some have Y.P.M.A's and were extremely jealous of anything that was to discipline them; others had literary societies and wanted nothing more; others yet thought that such a society had no business in our church; it was bringing in unorthodox methods and would teach young people cant and hypocrisy.[4]

There was concern within the Universalist General Convention at this suggestion as well. U.C.G. elders worried about a competitor of the General Convention for the loyalty of their young people. One of the U.G.C. executives was delegated to sit in on the first conference of the organizing committee to see that nothing dangerous was done.

In 1889 the Universalist General Convention held its General Assembly in Lynn, Massachusetts. The Lynn church had a strong young people's group which supported the idea of a Union. In conjunction with the young people from Michigan, this group organized a convention of young people on the day preceding the meeting of the U.G.C.

One hundred thirty-one delegates representing fifty-six soxieties from thirteen states were in attendence. On October 22, 1998, they hammered out a constitution and, after some controversy, chose to call themselves "The Young People's Christian Union of the Universalist Church". Walter Stuart Kelley, a delegate at the convention later recalled the debate over the name:

The most discussion developed over the name, with the contention that the word "Universalist" should be used : either Young People's Universalist Union (or Society) or Universalist Young People's Union. My argument for the name on the constitution as drafted was based upon two points: first, there was a good deal of misconception among orthodox people as to the religious state of the Universalist, and for that reason we should declare ourselves Christian; and second, the young people of the Congregational Church, in organizing the Christian Endeavor Society, had not seen fit to give it a denominational limitation, and I considered it a good precedent to follow. I made the concession of adding for ourselves—"of the Universalist Church" and with this the name was adopted by the Committee and by the convention."[5]

A Bay City man, Lee E. Joslyn, was elected first president of the Union, with James O. Tillinghast of Buffalo, N.Y. becoming secretary and Nannie Jemison of Lynn, Mass. treasurer. The Universalist Union became the official publication.

So the Young People's Christian Union (Y.P.C.U.) of the Universalist Church became the first self-initiated specifically denominational youth organization (in spite of Kelley's attraction to the Congregational example). It preceded and set an example for the Baptists, Lutherans, Methodists, and the Unitarians, who all followed suit within the next decade.

"Truth, Worship, and Service"[6]

The Young People's Religious Union (Y.P.R.U.) of the Unitarian Church did not come into being until 1896. Before this time there were three different groups within the American Unitarian Association competing against each other for members. One was the organization of Unity Clubs, mentioned above. In 1887 they had organized themselves into a National Bureau of Unity Clubs, with the well-known Unitarian leader, Edward Everett Hale, as their president. The National Bureau encouraged communication between the groups, and sponsored special events and lectures featuring Boston luminaries such as Julia Ward Howe.

In addition to his Unity Club work, Hale was also the originator of the "Lend-A-Hand Clubs", which mingled social activity with philanthropic work.

In 1887 a movement of "young people's guilds" began in a Unitarian society in Littleton, Massachusetts. The model for this third kind of group arose partly from the Christian Endeavor Societies, and partly from similar efforts being made in Unitarian and Anglican churches in England to create a program to bridge the gap between Sunday School and the adult church community. They too formed a National Alliance.

It was easy for some churches to have both a Guild and a Unity Club, for the Guilds tended to be worship-oriented and the Unity Clubs study-oriented. However, the Guilds were concentrated in the East and the Unity Clubs in the West. In 1890 the two national organizations joined together with the Unitarian Temperance Society to share a business agent at the American Unitarian Association headquarters in Boston, and to publish jointly a newspaper entitled Our Young People.

These national organizations were never very strong, although the local societies comprising them flourished. Then at the 1895 A.U.A. National Conference in Washington, D.C., a group of ministers conferred over the possibility of creating a single national union of young people's religious societies. They were concerned about the fact that although there was a strong youth work on the local level, there was a lack of any co-ordinated effort. Many local societies had clubs which were independent of any national affiliation.

The ministers decided to call a plenary meeting of all interested young people during the next Anniversary Week, May, 1896, in Boston. Arnold Crompton has written of the exhortations at that meeting:

It was Thomas Van Ness[7] who presented a plan whereby a national youth group could be formed around the ideals of worship, service, and truth. He attacked the prevailing attempts to hold young people in the churches by "pink teas", "oyster suppers", dancing parties, and dramatic shows. These were all right in their place, but should not be central. "We need to put before our young people high and strong ideals. They must be called upon to make personal exertion and to go out themselves to helpfulness and the regeneration of the world."[8]

On May 28, 1896, the Young People's Religious Union was founded. The delegates took "truth, worship, and service" as their cardinal principles and elected Thomas Van Ness as their first President. There were eighty-six local societies in the initial membership of the Y.P.R.U.

From the beginning both the Y.P.C.U. and the Y.P.R.U. were essentially self-governing. However, it would be deceiving to assign that fact the same weight it has today. At that time young people in the church were considered to be those under the age of thirty-five. The average age of the leadership in both organizations in those early days was well over thirty, and much of the early initiative and leadership came from young ministers. On the other hand, this is not to say that the tone and style of the youth organizations was completely identical to that of their parent bodies. Y.P.C.U. and Y.P.R.U. were created to fill a need. There were things that the young people thought they could do differently by working from a self-governing institutional base within the church.

"Two Cents A Week"

The first twenty years of the Young People's Christian Union were ones of growth. They probably represent the period of the Union's greatest strength. The Y.P.C.U. was formally composed of State Unions, and much

of the organizing effort that happened during those first few years went
on at the state level. For example, the Massachusetts-Rhode Island Union
had its membership leap in the first year from seventeen to fifty-eight
local unions. Membership statistics during this period are vague, however.
A safe estimate might be that at its peak during this period the Y.P.C.U.
had ten thousand active members. The best attended Y.P.C.U. National
Convention was in Boston in 1895. Six hundred delegates representing
two hundred thirty-nine unions in twenty-seven state were present.

The first annual National Convention of the Young People's Christian
Union was held in Rochester, N.Y. A major focus of that convention and of
Y.P.C.U. for many years after was missionary activity.

The story of the Y.P.C.U.'s early missionary thrust is one of the more
fascinating in the history of our youth movements. It does not seem to
have been initiated by the Y.P.C.U. members themselves, although they
quickly took it to their hearts. Initiatives and proddings from ministers
in attendance at the convention representing the Universalist church seems
to have started the ball rolling. The Reverend Charles Ellwood Nash and
Dr. Quillen Hamilton Shinn were the sparkplugs behind the decision to enter
the missionary field.[9]

The Rochester Convention of 1890 voted to build and support a
Universalist church in Harriman, Tennessee. Historians of that convention
are in disagreement about whether the idea to do so was first proposed by
Nash or by Harry Canfield, who was later to become Y.P.C.U.'s National
Secretary. At any rate, it seems clear that Nash had already begun the
Harriman work at the time. He had bought the land, and put some money
towards it. A letter written by Nash recalls the convention:

Thus far I had been almost solely responsible for the conduct of the
enterprise, and was debating in my own mind how to proceed further.

The inspiration came to me when I saw, and still more when I felt,
the spirit of the young people at the Rochester Convention. Thrilled
and elevated by the power of their own spiritual achievement and
ardently longing to render some more acceptable service to the
church of their faith, they were more than half ready to demand to
be shown some enterprise upon which they could concentrate to
display and demonstrate their purpose. I had only to propose that
they father the Harriman movement and the thing was done.

A thousand dollars was raised on the spot at the convention to support
the work. The initial money went to support a minister in Harriman, the
Rev. William H. McGlauflin. On Easter Sunday, 1892, the new church was
finished and dedicated. In one year the Union had raised some $6,000 to
support the construction, although the idea had caught fire in the
denomination and one general appeal had brought much of it in. All
totalled, the Y.P.C.U. put $8,000 into the Harriman venture.

In 1894 the Y.P.C.U. National Convention was held in Harriman,
Tennessee. It was reported to be a tremendously spirited convention,
boardering on the "pentecostal". Here Harry Canfield was elected National
Secretary. The Y.P.C.U. also created at this convention a "Junior Union",
aimed at high school age people and younger. Mary Grace Webb Canfield,
Harry's wife, became the first superintendent. The work of the Junior Unions
will be described further on. Another major event of the Harriman convention
was the inauguration of the "Two Cents A Week" Plan to raise money for
missionary work. The idea was to have every Y.P.C.U. member contribute
a dollar each year to this missionary fund. The name of the fund arose
from a comment by Charles Nash:

"Why, what is one dollar? It is only two cents a week for a year!"[11]

In the year 1893 Dr. Shinn was hired by the Y.P.C.U. as a national organizer. He devoted his time over the next few years to scouting out some likely places for missionary activity, and receiving and evaluating offers and requests for missionary work. Atlanta, Georgia became the next site to benefit from a Universalist church built by the Y.P.C.U. The union raised and contributed $16,000 to it, which was no mean sum at the turn of the century. Then Little Rock, Arkansas, was given $6,000 for a new chapel, and St. Paul, Minnesota had a new church constructed, (at a cost of $16,230) and called a new minister.

The peak of all this home mission activity was the construction of the Shinn Memorial Church in Chattanooga, Tennessee.[12] The first minister to serve the church, Luther Robinson, had been converted to Universalism by Y.P.C.U. literature. The 1916 National Convention was held at Chattanooga, and it was then that the church was dedicated.

The Y.P.C.U. also put $13,000 into the sponsorship of an itinerant Universalist preacher in Texas, "to send him abroad with a tent for his meetings," and to engage in "scripture proof-text" debates. "The fires of hell were literal and lurid in Texas theology." [13] Shinn also founded and the Y.P.C.U. supported a black Universalist church in Barton, Georgia. A black pastor, the Reverend John W. Murphy of Barton, had been converted to Universalism by the missionary literature.

There was a great deal of interest in Japan at that time, so Japan became the Y.P.C.U.'s focus for foreign missions. In 1904 the organization began contributing to the salary of a Japanese Universalist minister.

These programs of building and ministerial support were also accompanied by a Mission Study Program, which distributed books on mission work and carried on general evangelizing on that subject through the mails. A large Post Office Mission was also a part of the Y.P.C.U. program. For twenty-five years the union mailed out some twenty-five thousand tracts on Universalism each year to a mailing list of fifteen hundred.

The "Two Cents A Week" Plan continued very successfully until 1917. It resulted in the creation of a permanent fund for missions. The member's interest in the missions began to wane after the First World War. Attempts to revive the sagging fund were made over the next thirty years under various names (Home Mission, the Legion of the Cross, and finally Church Extension), but the enthusiasm of the early part of the century was never regained. However, the historical sketch published by the Union in 1939 showed that the Y.P.C.U. raised an average of $2,000 a year for missions during its fifty year history.

Early Projects and Problems in the Y.P.C.U.

The founding of the Y.P.C.U. Junior Unions in 1894 has been noted above. Mary Grace Canfield worked tremendously hard for the national Y.P.C.U. in encouraging the development of the Junior Unions. They grew to be an adjunct of the Sunday School, and often included people as young as fourteen. The Y.P.C.U.'s membership had a broader age range than that of the Y.P.R.U. from the beginning. In the first year after its founding, the national Junior Union boasted forty chapters. At peak strength there were 112 chapters with over 2,600 members. There was no substantial difference in the style and activity of the Junior Unions other than age. Activity surrounding mission work continued to be a major thrust.

Harry and Mary Canfield were central in this early Y.P.C.U. growth. Besides their administrative and organizing efforts, they co-edited the new national Y.P.C.U. publication, Onward. Another interesting personality of those days was Lucinda White Brown, or "Auntie Brown" as she was

affectionately called by Y.P.C.U.'ers. She was the widow of a Universalist
minister, the Rev. John Stanley Brown, of Akron, Ohio, and a friend to the
many Y.P.C.U.'ers, in her own area and at conventions of all kinds. When
she died, she left nearly $5,000 to the Y.P.C.U. which was the largest
single gift to the Union's endowment.

A recurrent political problem in the early days of the Y.P.C.U. was
the conflict of interest and power among the various state unions and the
national union, a conflict that is not unfamiliar to recent L.R.Y.'ers. Many
state unions were very strong, particularly in the East, where the great
majority of Universalist churches existed. The Massachusetts State Union,
for example, had been in favour of a national body, but from the beginning
considered that the cornerstone of membership and loyalty in Y.P.C.U. was
the state union. At its second annual meeting in 1890, the Massachusetts
State Union passed the following resolution:

> Resolved: that we favor a national union of young people's organizations,
> but feel that membership should be through state unions, and trust that
> the national union's constitution be so amended to allow such membership.[14]

Finances was one of the main points of controversy between the national
and state groups. The people who went as delegates to national conventions
would naturally get very inspired by the oratory of the speakers and by
the enthusiastic atmosphere. They would pledge dues, or gifts to Mission
work, far beyond the means of the groups back home. So the national
union would always find it necessary to dun the state unions for their dues,
and that created bad feelings. Other controversies had to do with over-
lapping offices and responsibilities among national and state officers,
and some overt political interference by national officers with state
meetings and elections.

The 1898 Y.P.C.U. convention held in Chicago proved to be somewhat of a watershed in resolving these disputes. The Massachusetts State Union spearheaded a drive to reduce the cost and influence of the National Union. The cost of putting out Onward was a particularly sore point, and in what became known as the "Chicago Plan", the Massachusetts delegation proposed to discontinue a salaried editor and secretary for Onward as well as other budget cuts. The measure passed, and the National Union carried on with more volunteer labor than before.

The Early Years of the Y.P.R.U.

There is less easily available documentation of the earliest years of the Young People's Religious Union than there is for the Y.P.C.U. In spite of claiming four thousand members in one hundred and sixteen affiliated groups by 1900, the national program was very low key. A part-time worker was employed by the Union to perform secretarial and administrative tasks at the outset. Only a dozen of these affiliated groups were outside of the New England and Middle Atlantic areas, so fund-raising for the Y.P.R.U. could be done via semi-annual bazaars in Boston. In addition, life memberships were sold at a cost of ten dollars each, and individual donations to the Union were solicited. There were one hundred seventy-eight life members on the rolls of the Y.P.R.U. by the 1930's when the practice of buying them had begun to die out.[15]

The Y.P.R.U. had a regular column in the Christian Register, and published a little journal called "Word and Work" in association with the A.U.A. and the Woman's Alliance. The Union did a certain amount of missionary work in its early days, but certainly nothing to compare with that of the Y.P.C.U. Financial contributions were made to struggling Unitarian churches in Dallas, Texas; Amherst, Massachusetts; and Pueblo,

Colorado.

In 1901 the first Young People's Day was held at the Isle of Shoals. This was only a day-long meeting but it marked the beginning of the Y.P.R.U.'s long association with the Shoals (commonly known today as Star Island). In 1902 the first District federations were formed along the lines of the A.U.A. District Conferences in Massachusetts, New York, New Jersey, Pennsylvania, and the city of Chicago.

Gradually the Y.P.R.U. was establishing itself on a firmer institutional base. The Union was incorporated in the Commonwealth of Massachusetts in 1911, and a formal declaration of trust for the Union funds was made. In its first major fund-raising campaign in 1914 the Union sought to establish a permanent endowment fund. A sum of $22,000 was raised, but the interest from that would only amount to $1100 a year.

"Shall We Ally Ourselves..?"

From the time that the Y.P.R.U. began, joint rallies were held with the Y.P.C.U. The first Uni-Uni rally was held in 1897 at the Universalists' Columbus Avenue Church in Boston. The rallies continued, and began a half-century of co-operation between the two groups on many levels, which eventually culminated in their merger.

Clinton Lee Scott, in his history of the Universalist Church, has documented the first discussion between the two groups of a joint program:

In 1897, the annual convention of the Y.P.C.U. was held in Detroit, Michigan. Rev. Jabez T. Sunderland was sent by the Unitarians as Y.P.C.U. fraternal delegate...Mr. Sunderland proposed to the Y.P.C.U. convention that in the future the two groups meet in joint convention. His suggestion, according to the report in Onward, was "greeted with cheers." There were, however, other opinions regarding this, and no

action was taken. Instead a resolution was passed extending
greetings to the Y.P.R.U. and "invoking the blessings of Almighty
God upon its endeavors after the Christian Life". Rev. Edwin C.
Sweetser of Philadelphia, a staunch denominationalist and author
of the pamphlet Shall We Ally Ourselves With the Unitarians? in
which he voiced an emphatic "no", was the delegate sent to the
Detroit meetings from the Universalist General Convention. He was
well qualified to speak for those in official positions who sought
to keep clear of entangling alliances."[16]

Union Programs

The fact that joint rallies were so quickly successful indicates that
there were not great differences between the activities and style of the
two groups on the local level. The groups were by and large affiliated
with one local church although it appears that in this regard "youth-adult
relations" have changed little over the years. One history of a Y.P.C.U.
State Union noted:

The Board had met with a number of disappointments, especially in
the number of churches which had denied them the privilege of
meeting; but the Board overcame all such difficulties."[17]

Sunday meetings in both groups would generally consist of some topic
for discussion, or perhaps a speaker. Many of the notable Universalist
leaders in the Boston area, such as Clarence Skinner or A.A. Miner, would
take the time to address local union meetings. The evening's topic would
be followed by a business session if necessary, and then would often end
with a short worship service.

The Y.P.C.U. appears to have been more devotional than the Y.P.R.U.
The Universalist local unions would often have meetings revolving around

an evening of worship. Harry Adams Hersey, the historian of the Y.P.C.U.'s

first half-century, observed:

"It could not have been organized if the religious program had been

omitted...The heart is not strangely warmed at socials, however laudable

and necessary, at dances, however well-conducted, or in money-raising

enterprises, however proper and fruitful."[18]

There was a pietistic group, a kind of "Oxford Movement" within the

early Y.P.C.U. It was called "The Comrades of the Quiet Hour". This was

a group of people particularly interested in personal religious life and

devotion.

Perhaps the most striking differences between those early conventions

and the L.R.Y. conferences of today can be found in the menus. They

certainly knew how to eat then. Witness the menu for the Massachusetts

State Y.P.C.U. Annual Banquet of 1904:

MENU

"The turnpike road to people's hearts, I find
Lies thro' their mouth, or I mistake mankind."
                              -Dr. Wolcott

ESSCALLOPED OYSTERS

"Now if you're ready oysters dear..."   -Carroll

MEATS

I do perceive here a divine duty -"   -Othello

TURKEY AND CRANBERRY SAUCE
HAM   TONGUE
CHICKEN CROQUETTES
AND PEAS

"Bid them cover the table, serve in the meat-"
                              -Merchant of Venice
"Don't talk all the talk, nor eat all the meat"
                              -Proverb

SALADS

CHICKEN   POTATO   LOBSTER
"Yet shall you have to rectify your palate
on olive, capers, or some better salad."
                              -Ben Jonson

ICE CREAM

STRAWBERRY   VANILLA   CHOCOLATE
"A mockery King of Snow"   -King Richard

SHERBETS

ORANGE   RASPBERRY
"A little snow, tumbled about"   -King John

CAKE
"Couldst thou both eat thy cake and have it"
                          -Herbert

COFFEE
"Tis strong, and it does indifferent well"
                      -Twelfth Night

ROLLS
"Better half a loaf than no bread"   -Camden

OLIVES
"If at first you don't succeed, try,try,try again."[19]

The first World War in a way represents the end of the initial growth period of our denominational youth organizations. By the beginning of the war, both were fairly well-established and relatively stable both in finances and membership. The war years were a time of reduced activity, for many young people went off to fight with the support and encouragement of their Y.P.C.U. and Y.P.R.U. friends back home. However, the regular Y.P.R.U. columns in The Christian Register indicate that local chapters continued to function strongly.

The times were changing quickly. There is a brief note at the end of the minutes of a 1912 Y.P.C.U. Annual Convention:

The convention adjourned at 12:15 and the afternoon was spent at an outing at Wading River Farm, Marshfield, where lunch was served. The highpoint of the convention was the fact that the outing was made in automobiles.[20]

When activity began to gear up again after the war, it was already a new world.

LUCIE HARMON REMEMBERS TOLEDO, OHIO - 1890's

The Eight O'Clock Club, while not a part of the Sunday School grew out of it and was for several years(during the 1890's) a flourishing institution well loved by us in our late teens and early twenties. It's members were Toledo, Ohio Unitarians and our friends who attended other churches or none at all. We met on Monday evenings in the church parlor.

The programs, and they were often lively, consisted of music, re-citations, dissertations on various subjects, debates. There were usually 25 or more present and it didn't take refreshments to bring them out, for there were none. It just satisfied the natural desire of young people for sociability.

The Eight O'Clockers were older than me. Three or four years make a big difference at that age, so we formed another Sunday School class and had our own little social club which met regularly in one anothers homes with some outsiders who were not Unitarians. But we were not as high minded as the Eight O'Clockers for it took refreshments and prizes to hold us together.

After several years of happy and enthusiastic association the Eight O'Clockers disintegrated, and I believe this was due to the sudden and untimely death of Harry Boss. He and Gus Fenneberg were devoted friends and leaders in the club. Harry's death cast a spirit of gloom over all from which the club never recovered.

Another interesting if ephemeral outgrowth of the Sunday School was the attempt made by Lydia Commander and Beth Cummings to establish a branch of the Young People's Religious Union. This must have occured about 1903. John Haynes Holmes was at that time studying at Harvard and came to Toledo for this purpose. Bert met him at the station and brought him to our

house where a group had assembled. After supper we went to the church
where Mr. Holmes went competently to work and organized us into a branch
of the Y.P.R.U.

At a later meeting I was assigned to speak on "What Jesus Means
To Me". Although I was teaching school at the time and should have
possessed some sense and ability, this seemed like an impossible task
and I am sure the results were far from inspiring.

Normal Unitarian young people were not used then, if they are now,
to offering prayer or exposing their innermost beliefs on religious subjects.
And so the Toledo branch of the Y.P.R.U. died aborning, in spite of its
now famous founder.

VINCENT SILLIMAN REMEMBERS MEADVILLE, PA.-1915

My first real contact with Unitarian youth activities was the Young People's Religious Union of the Unitarian Church in Meadville, Pennsylvania. I arrived in Meadville in 1915, and attended the group regularly for a year or two. The membership was high school age and up. Other Meadville students attended. I was twenty-one at the time.

Total attendence at meetings must have been around 25 at least. Nelson Julius Springer, a Meadville student, was president of the Meadville Y.P.R.U., at least some of the time I attended it. He had briefly been an actor before attending Meadville, and used to preside at meetings dressed in full evening dress, and wearing white gloves that, as I recall, could have been whiter than they were.

A meeting consisted of a service from the youth hymnal Jubilate Deo, by Charles W. Wendte, led by the president. Then we had an outside speaker. I don't clearly recall any other activity. The church organist Minnie Gibson, played the piano. There may have been an occasional dance, though I doubt it.

KATHERINE HOOKE REMEMBERS DORCHESTER, MA. -1918

It was some 60-odd years ago in Dorchester, Mass. that I became a member of the Nathaniel Hall Society of the First Parish Church. This young people's society was considered by some to be one of the outstanding Y.P.R.U. (Young People's Religious Union) groups in the country at the time.

What was it like to be a part of that group? It was to look forward eagerly from one meeting to the next. Twice a month there was a Sunday evening devotional service with a speaker - planned and conducted by the members and often attended by a few interested adults. Once a month there was a business meeting followed by a social evening. The business was conducted with careful adherence to Roberts' Rules of Order and frequently decisions became very complex; the social evening consisted largely of dancing and good fellowship.

In those days Hi-Fi had not been developed, nor had small orchestras become important to us. We were satisfied to hire a pianist for the season and had just as much fun. Sometimes, for a special party, like the annual masquerade, we would add a drum and traps. That made for a gala occasion with a surprising variety of costumes and much enthusiasm. The social committee always secured two mothers as chaperones, and the young people were careful to greet them at the beginning and say good-night to them at the end of the evening. There was nothing forced about this recognition of an accepted social custom of those days.

Once a year the "Nat Hall Society" as it was affectionately called (named for a former minister) planned and staged a dramatic performance which ran for two nights. Plays such as "The Geisha Girl", "The Importance of Being Ernest", "The Dover Road", "Charlie's Aunt", etc. succeed in bolstering the treasury that the Society could carry out its social service

---

work: providing Thanksgiving baskets for needy persons, making Christmas for a family of children who would have had none, occasionally visiting shut-ins, etc. The Treasury was also used to send delegates to the Isle of Shoals conferences. In addition to the cast there was stage managing, lighting, advertising, publicity and programming to be done by other members. -Participation which strengthened the organization.

Sunday afternoon hikes, picnics (sometimes even in winter) and other impromptu gatherings were common. We belonged to and were active in the Boston Federation of the Y.P.R.U. societies and attended monthly meetings in large numbers. That was before young people had their own cars. Therefore, it was necessary to use public transportation to get to meetings; sometimes an hour's trip each way with one or two transfers. It was a lark! Because we had fun being together. And, because we attended these meetings and other district conferences in such large numbers, we became acquainted with other Y.P.R.U. groups and were able to take part in their activities, too. Many of us became active in the Federation dramatics which were staged in Boston. For many of us "Nat Hall" was the basis of our social life, as well as a wonderful experience in taking responsibility and learning how to run an organization whose membership fluctuated from about 35 to 50.

Y.P.R.U. Sunday was observed annually with our members conducting the entire service-two or more in the pulpit (one preaching the sermon), one as organist, a choir of 10 or 12 and 4 ushers.

I suppose our average individual membership lasted only 4 or 5 years. One had to be 15 years old to join, and then the beginning of college marked a change in interests. However, several members (commuters to college) continued active membership when they could, and the Christmas and Spring vacations brought about joyful reunions. Membership was not restricted to Unitarians but was open to interested friends.

Our activities were not limited to our own organization. There
was excellent rapport with the adults of the church who were interested
in what we were doing and who welcomed our participation in their
activities - suppers, fairs, etc. Many of us were regular attendants
at church services - another opportunity to be together - and when the
50th anniversary of the Nathaniel Hall Society was observed in the early
1960s, there was a surprising turn-out, some members coming from a
considerable distance to attend the dinner following church service.

We loved our organization and gave much of ourselves to it. In
return we gained life-time friendships, and some even found their life
partners.

Perhaps the most distinguishing characteristic of the Nathaniel Hall
Society was its esprit de corps. This was a heritage from previous
members and was carefully nurtured by all of us.

Chapter 2: BUILDING THE INSTITUTION

The new world after World War I brought with it a new generation of
leadership in Unitarian and Universalist youth organizations, and the
establishment of a firm institutional foundation which insured the survival
of the youth movement as a distinctive branch of the liberal church.

The Y.P.R.U.'s financial campaign before the war began was the first
step towards changing the program from the Boston area corresponding
secretariat that it had been up until that time. In 1917, the organization
hired its first Field Secretary in an attempt to reach out to member groups
further away from Boston.

The leaders of both the Y.P.R.U. and the Y.P.C.U. at this time were
still people in their early thirties, all of them working, many of them
married. Frederick Eliot was the Y.P.R.U. president as the war ended, while
the Universalists had just elected Helen Bisbee, the first woman to be
president of the Y.P.C.U.[1]

A Campaign for Cash

The Young People's Religious Union at this time was governed by a
group of elected officers and a board of eighteen directors, who were
elected in groups of six for three year terms. Regional committees
functioned more as subcommittees of this central administration. Regions
could send voting representatives to Y.P.R.U. Board Meetings, however.

This was hardly a "continental" or even a national board. Although
fifteen regions representing two hundred twenty-eight local societies [2]
were involved, it was still very New England oriented. The monthly board
meetings were always held in Boston, and since no travel subsidies were
paid, only New Englanders came. Robert Raible,[3] in personal correspondence,
describes his frustration at attending a Y.P.R.U. Board Meeting in 1923,

seeking to represent a region where he was among the recognized leaders
of the youth program. He was allowed to sit in, but not to participate,
in spite of the fact that no other representatives had been able to attend.

The early 1920's saw the first major shift in the age of the Y.P.R.U.'s
leadership from an average age over thirty to completely under thirty.
Robert Raible writes:

I can recollect Charles Bolster and Ed Furber[4] being Presidents of

Y.P.R.U. after they were married (which means they were somewhere around

thirty). I do not recollect exactly. I do remember trying to run

an abortive campaign against Charles Bolster for Y.P.R.U. President

on the sole ground that a married man was too old to be President

of Y.P.R.U.[5]

The paid staff during the twenties consisted of one full-time
Executive Secretary in Boston (who started with a salary of seven hundred
dollars per year), assisted by up to four field secretaries, located in
New England, the Middle Atlantic, the Midwest, and the Pacific Coast areas.
This expansion in staff was made possible by a huge fund-raising drive
sponsored by the American Unitarian Association entitled The Unitarian
Campaign. The Campaign was begun in 1920. It was designed to be a united
fund-raising effort on behalf of twelve Unitarian-related organizations.
Over a five year period The Unitarian Campaign raised around two million,
four hundred thousand dollars, for the A.U.A. and its affiliates.

The Y.P.R.U. had to demonstrate to the board of prominent Unitarians
managing the campaign that it had a program and a plan for the future worth
supporting. One of the main arguments in their applications hinged around
the developing interest within Unitarian circles in "student work", i.e.
programming for college students. The Y.P.R.U. argued that this area should
be under their program, and could be effectively handled if only the

organization was given the money to carry out a program.

The young people ended up receiving considerably less than they had asked for from the Unitarian Campaign, but the money that was donated made a substantial difference.

An initial donation of five thousand dollars in 1921 was used to pull the organization out of a deficit situation and to expand the staff to include an office secretary and new field workers. The Endowment Fund Drive of 1914 had been an attempt to establish a permanent guaranteed annual budget for Y.P.R.U., since the contributions of affiliated groups would pay for only a small percentage of the kind of program the Y.P.R.U. wanted to have. Donations from The Unitarian Campaign increased the size of the endowment to fifty thousand dollars by 1925. The interest from this sum was still not enough to free Y.P.R.U. from the necessity of fund-raising, however.

Young People's Week

One of the most enduring youth programs within our denomination from the early days right up until the present has been Youth Sunday. The first "Young People's Day" was held by the Young People's Christian Union of the Universalist Church on January 31, 1892. The idea was propagated far and wide among Y.P.C.U. groups, but the Unitarians were quite slow picking it up from them. However, when they did it quickly became an annual institution. A 1931 Y.P.R.U. handbook describes the origins of Young People's Week:

It was in 1917 that the idea of Young People's Sunday was first conceived by Rev. Houghton Page, one of the many Unitarian ministers who at that time began to show a real interest in the activities of our Y.P.R.U. He requested that the first Sunday

in December be observed as Young People's Day in all Unitarian
churches, and that the young people be allowed to take a prominent
part in the church services. The response at that time was small,
and it was not until 1921 that the officers of the Y.P.R.U.,
realizing the infinite possibilities of Mr. Page's suggestion,
began to campaign, first with and then through the individual
members of the organization for the observance of Young People's
Day as an annual event in our churches.

In 1921, about a hundred churches observed it in some way,
and in about forty churches the local members of the Y.P.R.U. took
part in or took charge of the service. Each year the response has
been greater, and as the young people have proved beyond a doubt
their growing interest, power, and capability in the work of our
churches, the feeling of skepticism on the part of the ministers
and the church members has diminished until now Young People's Sunday
is observed annually by at least two-thirds of our churches, and is
looked forward to, not as something to be endured for the sake of
the young folk, but something to be enjoyed with them.

Young People's Sunday in Boston became the beginning of the annual
Young People's Week, which included parties, fund-raising events, a
dance, and a play with a Y.P.R.U. cast that was presented downtown and
in several suburbs. Young People's Week developed into a major fund-
raiser for the Union.

Y.P.C.U. Programs and Prospects

The financial troubles and political controversies which existed
within the Y.P.C.U. between the national and the state unions, and which
had occasioned the watershed 1898 convention in Chicago, gradually became

less and less acute. By 1910, the finances particularly had improved, and a full-time secretary for field work was appointed. Roger Etz was his name and he made a success of the job. Etz went on to become Superintendent of the Universalist General Convention. The position of Field Secretary continued under Carl Elsner and after him Stanley Manning, who was officially appointed Director of Young People's work within the U.G.C. in 1919.

The organization of the Y.P.C.U. at this time was similar to the L.R.Y. structure of the sixties, within a much smaller geographic scale. There was a national board which governed the affairs of the Y.P.C.U., and working for it was one full-time person, centered in Boston, but with a mandate to travel. During and after World War I, a certain drop in size and activity of the membership was experienced, as one might expect. One of the eventual consequences was a move towards merger among some of the smaller state unions. The small Rhode Island Union, for example, joined the stronger Massachusetts Union in 1926.

The old "Two Cents a Week" Plan for missions kept up its head of steam. In 1922, Clifford and Margaret Stetson, two Universalist missionaries who were members of and sponsored by the Y.P.C.U. went over to Japan, and remained for nine years. The Junior Unions later supported the education of some Japanese girls through the Stetsons. As has been noted above, the name "Two Cents A Week" was changed in 1917 to "Home Mission", with the hope that a new image might revive it. "Home Mission" proved a little too lack-lustre, so later on that year the name "Legion of the Cross" was settled on.

The Y.P.C.U.'s finances were somewhat more stringent after the war ended. Much hope was placed in the Universalist General Convention's

ambitious 1919 campaign for funds, unabashedly entitled "The Million Dollar
Drive". The U.G.C. got its million, and henceforth supported the Y.P.C.U.'s
budget to the tune of fifty percent. Additional support was forthcoming
too, particularly when the Union experienced financial difficulties. Onward,
the Y.P.C.U. publication, was in constant financial trouble, and varied
from a sixteen page weekly to a sporadic newsletter. The Universalist
Publishing House occasionally pumped a little money into it.

The membership of the Y.P.C.U. after the war levelled off at between
four and five thousand, although exact figures are hard to determine. The
Universalist group experienced a similar slow drop in age during the 1920's
as did its Unitarian counterpart. Harry Adams Hersey noted that the
average age of a Y.P.C.U. Board member in 1895 was twenty-nine and a half
years old. In the early days of the Union, when they were running four
or five churches, paying ministers' salaries, carrying on the Post Office
Mission, etc., the leadership of the Y.P.C.U. consisted of ministers or
prominent laypeople in their late twenties or early thirties. As these
responsibilities gradually fell away, it became apparent that the members
of the organization (who were generally younger than the leadership) might
respond more favourably to leaders of their own age. The Ferry Beach
convention of the Y.P.C.U. in 1919 had seen the first influx of what was
described as "very young" people, i.e. people in their teens. What Hersey
called "the epoch of youth only" was beginning.[6]

Summer Conferences and Conventions

The backbone of the youth program in our denomination has always been
the summer conferences. Without that conference experience many of the
local youth groups and certainly the regional and continental organizations
would have withered like leaves on a dead tree.

The first weekend conference sponsored by the Young People's Religious Union at the Isle of Shoals (Star Island) off the coast of Portsmouth, New Hampshire, was held in 1921. The response to the longer conference was favorable, and since the Union was back on its feet financially as a result of the Unitarian Campaign, it was decided to try a week-long conference in 1922. The response was overwhelming. Two hundred fifty delegates, including many from outside New England, were in attendance. The experience of that week had a far-reaching effect in the Unitarian churches. In 1923 the Young People's Conference was expanded to two full weeks, and the Y.P.R.U. Annual Meeting was held in conjunction with the conference. So began a tradition of Y.P.R.U. National Conferences at Star Island which was not broken until 1940.

The Young People's Christian Union had long sponsored extended summer camps and conventions for young people at such places as Ferry Beach, in Saco, Maine, and Murray Grove, New Jersey. The National Convention was moved around from year to year, and such far-flung places as Chicago, Minneapolis, Detroit, and even Los Angeles became National Convention sites. This was quite a contrast to the Unitarians, for whom Young People's Week at The Shoals became a kind of Mecca.

Other conferences were initiated out of the success of The Shoals experience, however. The districts sponsored mid-year and spring weekend conferences, and by 1924 there were five other week-long summer conferences: one at Rowe Camp in western Massachusetts, two in the Midwest, and two in California, which led eventually to the founding of a California District Y.P.R.U.

The relationship of the Young People's Religious Union to Rowe Camp is an interesting one, for the founding and growth of Rowe was intimately tied with a desire and need for young people's summer camps in Western

Massachusetts and Connecticut. When official Y.P.R.U. summer conferences began to be held at Rowe, the president of the Y.P.R.U. was asked to sit in as an ex-officio member of the Rowe board. The National Y.P.R.U. received its first unrestricted bequest from the estate of a Deerfield, Massachusetts resident, who had maintained a long interest in and affection for the young people's programs at Rowe.

Lucy E. Henry died on Young People's Sunday in 1927. She left some small bequests to institutions in the town of Rowe itself,[7] but a substantial amount of the estate, amounting to one-half of the residue after other bequests and expenses had been met, was left to the Young People's Religious Union. It amounted to $1,235.79.

The year after Miss Henry's death, Unitarian Rowe Camp, Inc. decided to purchase the Bonnie Blink Cottage and the land upon which it stood to establish the camp as a permanent institution. The original deed to the camp land specified that in the event of the dissolution of Unitarian Rowe Camp, Inc. the title should revert to the Young People's Religious Union. In view of the fact that Miss Henry's bequest came as a result of "the Rowe Spirit" and in view of the decision to purchase the camp land, the Y.P.R.U. Board elected to donate one half of the bequest back to Rowe for the possible construction of a dining hall.

By 1934 the Rowe summer conference was so successful that there was fear of it rivalling the National Convention at The Shoals. The two conferences were carefully scheduled at different times.

These early conferences and conventions had the same occasional problems with rules that today's conferences have. Dana Greeley recalls one flap at Star Island regarding conferees hauling their mattresses out onto the roof of the Oceanic Hotel in order to be able to sleep outside.[8] The conventions and the summer camps also provided the same unusual

opportunities for young people to travel, as they do today. A convention
was an occasion for months of saving and fund-raising climaxed by an
exciting train trip, since the state delegations would often gather
together and take one train. The long expensive trips to conventions
stirred up some controversy then as now. Harry Adams Hersey had some
sharp replies to such criticism in his fiftieth anniversary memoir of the
Young People's Christian Union:

> Hundreds of thousands of dollars for travelling expenses and joy
> riding! Why this waste? Might they not better have stayed home,
> and given the money to the church or to missions? The answer is
> that, first, the money would not have been given, and second, it
> it that our young people knew a good investment when they saw one.
> No money ever spent by our young people produced richer returns.
> Before travel was possible for most of our youth, in the ordinary
> course of life, the conventions made it possible; opened up new
> worlds, broadened the mind, quickened the sympathies, enlarged
> the interests, benefitted the whole man, and blessed ultimately the
> whole denomination.[9]

The Student Federation of Religious Liberals

As has been noted above, "student work" began to be an area of
greater concern for the youth program during the 1920's. In conjunction
with a joint A.U.A.-Y.P.R.U campaign to establish young people's societies
in every church, a Joint Student Committee was created in 1923. It was
composed of representatives from the A.U.A., the Alliance of Women, the
Unitarian Ministerial Union, the Layman's League, and the Y.P.R.U. Its
task was to avoid duplication of efforts and to collectively promote student
work.

There were a good many college students involved in the Y.P.C.U. and
the Y.P.R.U., and there existed various "Channing Clubs" and other Y.P.R.U.
branches on campuses. However, no effort was made to creat an organization
to specifically address the needs of college students until 1923, when the
Student Federation of Religious Liberals (S.F.R.L.) was created.[10]

The instigator was, predictably enough, a minister. He was an
Englishman, and the minister of King's Chapel in Boston: the Reverend
Harold B. Speight. Speight was instrumental in having the second week of
the 1923 Shoals Young People's Convention be declared a "Student Week".
The idea of a program directed at college students alone was Speight's
pet project, and he managed to sell it to the two hundred sixty-five
liberal religious students (representing seventy-five schools from twenty
states and Canada) that were assembled on the island. Robert Raible
became the first president of the fledgling organization, heading up an
eleven-person executive committee. Alfred Hobart was appointed as a full-
time paid Executive Secretary. Speight went down to the fall meeting of
the Unitarian General Conference that year looking for funding, and he came
back with a promise of financial support for S.F.R.L.

Both Y.P.R.U. and Y.P.C.U. decided to lend financial and moral support
as well. S.F.R.L. became a federation of the Y.P.R.U., with two repressen-
tatives on their board. The organization began with eight affiliated member
groups and thirty-one individual members.

Alfred Hobart travelled extensively to many colleges during that first
year of adequate funding, then left the job for higher pursuits at the
Meadville Theological School. Raible took over the Executive Secretary
job, but the organization could only afford him half-time. Granville Hicks,
a prominent Y.P.C.U. leader and editor of Onward, served as President during
that second year. S.F.R.L. produced The Student Leader, a monthly four page

glossy newsletter, and also distributed _Onward_. The Executive Secretary
also corresponded with and distributed material on the Leyden International
Bureau, an international corresponding secretariat of liberal religious
young people based in Holland. This represented the first contact the
North Americans had with the attempts in Europe to bring liberal religious
youth together across national boundaries.

Speight was never again as successful in raising money from denominational sources for the venture as he had been during that first year.
The second annual S.F.R.L. conference at Mount Holyoke Collage drew one
hundred fifty students from forty schools, and included Congregationalists,
Friends, and Episcopalians. Towards the end of the second year, the
crushing blow came. Y.P.R.U. became disenchanted with the program, and,
suspicious about the number of non-Unitarians in S.F.R.L.'s membership,
severed its funding. When Russell Wood became the third president of
S.F.R.L., there was too little money left to hire a secretary, and he did
all the office work as well.

In 1926, the Student Federation of Religious Liberals was disbanded.
It had managed to hold three annual conferences: 1923 at Star Island,
1924 at Mt. Holyoke, and 1925 at Phillips Andover Academy. It was a
valiant try, and one that would not be attempted again on any national
scale for twenty years.

A Financial Crunch

As the 1920's ended, both youth groups began to feel pressured for
funds again. The Unitarian Campaign money had expired in 1925. A new drive
was begun in that year under the name "Unitarian Foundation". Young people
responded enthusiastically to the drive. When the Star Island Convention
of that year was told of the efforts, spontaneous pledges totalling $1,237.00

were made by some two hundred young people within three hours.

The Foundation pledged a ten thousand dollar grant to the Y.P.R.U. for 1927, which no one really expected it to receive. A sum of four thousand dollars was budgeted, but in the end only $2,504.50 was given.

It was necessary to conduct a special appeal to pay off the 1927 debts, and to cut back in the budget as well. Two field secretaryships were amalgamated into one, and Y.P.R.U. sounded out the Laymen's League on the possibility of sharing the expenses and time of the more far-flung field workers. The Y.P.R.U. Magazine, Pegasus, which had been under-subscribed since its inception in 1926, also had to be cut back.

As the year 1929 began it was apparent that Foundation monies were exhausted. The Y.P.R.U. and the Layman's League decided to embark upon a joint fund-raising effort as a demonstration of co-operative fund-raising, and as a last ditch effort to establish a permanent endowment which could meet Y.P.R.U.'s annual budget needs in perpetuity.

This campaign was entitled the "Maintenance Fund". Its goal was four hundred six thousand dollars was to go into the Y.P.R.U. endowment. Then in October, 1929, the stock market crashed. Although many Unitarian and Universalist churches lost heavily, the Y.P.R.U. and the Y.P.C.U. were not badly hurt. The effect of the crash and the Depression was to be felt more slowly over the course of the 1930's. The Depression did bring an end to the Maintenance Fund, however. It was the last major fund-raising effort of its kind.

CHARLES S. BOLSTER REMEMBERS BROOKLINE, MA - 1920's

From 1921 until about 1929 I was a member (and at one time President) of the Lyon Guild, which was the official name of the young people's group in the First Parish in Brookline, Massachusetts. The meetings were usually business affairs: arranging programs, assisting the church where possible, etc. Each year the group put on a dramatic production in the hall adjacent to and part of the church. Also each spring the group went on a Sunday afternoon and evening picnic at the country or seashore homes of parents.

During the winter, we had Sunday evening meetings preceded by suppers which were prepared by members. I remember I became noted for strawberry shortcake, made from scratch in the church kitchen on Sunday afternoon. I fear that the group's activities were chiefly on the social side rather than the religious or ecclesiastical.

Before that, I was a member of the "Fraternity" at All Souls Church in Roxbury, the activities of which were similar to those described above.

In 1926, 1927, and 1928 I was President of the national Y.P.R.U., the duties of which took all my available time so that I did not participate in local society activities after that, other than visiting different local societies, chiefly in New England, but on a few occasions in the Midwest and New York areas. I preached the sermon on three successive youth Sundays at Brookline, Jamestown, N.Y., and Billerica, Massachusetts and was active in connection with the Y.P.R.U. summer conferences, chiefly at Star Island.

I then believed and still believe that if young people (and by that I mean in ages from 17 or 18 to 23 or 24) can organize a group closely affiliated with a church, and if that group can assemble at monthly gatherings, such activities strengthen the life of the members and also the corporate life of the church. I know that my experiences in the Lyon

Guild, and later in the National Y.P.R.U. work meant a great deal to me and enriched my life as much as anything I did then.

CONARD AND ANN RHEINER REMEMBER WAKEFIELD, MA - 1920's

Ann: I was a member of the Y.P.C.U. at the First Universalist Church of

Wakefield, Mass. from 1922 to 1927. It was a very small group of

young people. Mostly the minister helped to form Y.P.C.U.'s, and

in our case he was our consultant.

We formed an organization, held elections for officers, chose

committees for worship services, a Y.P.C.U. representative in the New

England organization, a Social Committee and fund-raising chairman.

We raised our own budget, including $500 each year for the last two

years during which I was a member, which we raised for the church.

We met on Sunday nights. The programs were part devotional, and

part educational. Every person in the group took a turn being the

speaker, and then we brought in outsiders.

Con :   We were married at the Wakefield Church. I was a student at

Tufts, and one of my fellow students was the president of the Wakefield

Y.P.C.U. He knew that I'd had plenty of experience as an actor, and

that I was a professional magician, and entertainer, and so he hired me

for fifty dollars to be in their play. That was a considerable amount

of money at the time, although it represented eight trips to Wakefield.

That's where we met.

Ann: In about 1920 we pledged to raise $500 towards the budget of the

church. We did it by giving these plays - three a year, running for

three nights each. We also got permission to have social dancing in

the downstairs vestry because this town of 15,000 had a dance hall

with a bad name.

We participated in the New England organization of Y.P.C.U.'s and co-operated with the national office in Boston.

We had anywhere from 50 to 75 people at these conventions. I'll never forget the first one I went to at Concord, New Hampshire. My present sister-in-law and I (we were chums then) were placed in a home of one of the prominent people in the church. We had the most beautiful bedroom, and breakfast brought to us in bed the next morning with a rose on the tray.

Con: You have to put that period in perspective because there was nothing to compete. We did have movies, and we did have dance halls, but middle class families frowned upon their children going to dance halls. No radio, no television.

Ann: I remember the church Board of Trustees up in arms about the fox trot, and the tango.

Something else we did in Wakefield was , we initiated an organization made up of young people's groups from the Congregationalist, Methodist, Baptist, and Episcopal churches, that met once a month for an ecumenical worship service, a "sing-together", and once to put on a play: "The Admirable Creighton" by James M. Barrie in the High School Auditorium.

I was just thinking, as we worked on the plans for our 50th wedding anniversary, how many of those people we have kept in touch with over all these years. Y.P.C.U. meant a great deal to us.

Con: And three out of the young people's group that I was in are in the U-U ministry today. And two out of Ann's group.

Chapter 3:   CO-OPERATION AT HOME AND ABROAD

The year 1929 was, not unexpectedly, one of financial difficulty
within the Young People's Christian Union. The organizational strength
of the Y.P.C.U. was not concentrated in a few urban areas as was the case
with the Unitarians. The Universalist organization was somewhat more spread
out and could not rely on its own fund-raising activities or donations
from the mother church as Y.P.R.U. had begun to do. The money had to
come in from the state and local unions and it was not coming.

The 1929 Y.P.C.U. Convention was held in Atlanta, Georgia. Dorothy
Tilden Spoerl was elected President that year of a Union that was forced
to make serious cutbacks, particularly in its budget for the publication
of Onward. The buildup to the convention was notable for the fact that
one faction of the Y.P.C.U. was strongly pushing for an organic union
with the Y.P.R.U. as a final solution to the Union's financial problems.

Overtures to Merger

Speculation about a possible merger of the Y.P.R.U. and the Y.P.C.U.
was quite common during this period. In 1927 the two organizations took
up the practice of exchanging delegates to their respective conventions.
This had been quite common in the earliest days, but had become more
sporadic during the first World War.

In 1927-28 the two Unions also held conferences of their national
officers to compare notes on subjects of mutual interest and to discuss
future co-operation. The suggestion of organic union of the two groups
came from the Universalist side in proposals published in Onward in 1928-
29. There was opposition to the idea, and the Unitarians displayed no
great enthusiasm for it, although the conversation about the possibility
continued. No decisions were reached at the summer conferences of 1929,

but during the following year a joint committee of six evaluated the idea.
The committee invited forty Unitarian and Universalist young people to a
series of meetings to discuss the matter. The meetings proved inconclusive
and no decision was reached. The idea was laid to rest for another few
years.

During the early thirties Dana Greeley and Max Kapp were the Presidents
of the Y.P.R.U. and the Y.P.C.U. respectively. Both would later be involved
in the final Unitarian-Universalist merger, and would work together within
the same U.U.A. administration. Greeley recalls that his first serious
reflections on the real possibilities of Unitarian-Universalist merger
happened in the context of the youth movement. He remembers meeting with
Kapp and others in the home of John Van Schaick, the editor of the Universalist journal, The Christian Leader, and talking long into the night about
the implications of a merger. [1]

The A.U.A. and the Universalist General Convention at this time had
appointed commissions on interdenominational relations and were entertaining
the idea of establishing a "Free Church of America". [2] This was not to be an
A.U.A. - U.G.C. merger as such, but a wider union of religious liberals of
various faiths.

With Dana Greeley as President, the Y.P.R.U. set up its own Committee
on Interdenominational Relations, which made a variety of recommendations
for closer co-operation between the Y.P.R.U. and the Y.P.C.U. The Committee
favored parallel commissions within these two youth organizations to "formulate
a plan or plans for progressive co-operation and to apply to young people's
work to the extent practicable the plan of the Free Church of America". The
Free Church of America died a-borning, but the enthusiasm that existed
around it was a valuable impetus in the direction of increased co-operation.

One important positive step in that direction was taken in 1933 with the establishment of a Joint Commission on Social Responsibility. Other recommendations made by the Committee on Interdenominational Relations involved membership overlap and co-operation where only one of the groups existed in a given area. They suggested that only one group be formed where none had existed before. Joint attendance at all summer conferences was also recommended and consideration was given to merging the Y.P.C.U.'s Onward with the Y.P.R.U. News.

Clinton Lee Scott describes a further flurry of merger activity later in the thirties:

> The next definite action came from the Unitarian group. William E.
> Gardner, in an article in the Christian Leader of August 17,1935,
> reported that "the Y.P.R.U., at its annual meeting in May, 1935,
> voted to effect an organic union with the Y.P.C.U. if the Y.P.C.U.
> so desired." Reports from the Y.P.C.U. convention held at Ferry
> Beach, Maine that July gave evidence that the Universalist youth
> also desired merger, but under pressure from denominational officials
> action was "postponed" until another year.[3]

The Peace Caravans

One of the social responsibility projects that members of both the Y.P.R.U. and the Y.P.C.U. became involved in at this time is particularly interesting. With the help of the American Friends Service Committee and Robert Dexter, Executive Secretary of the A.U.A.'s Department of Social Relations, a Y.P.R.U. - Y.P.C.U. Peace Caravan was sponsored over the five summers between 1931 and 1935.

"Peace " was a rubric which encompassed many of the international issues of the early thirties. The international arms buildup, the ineffectiveness of the League of Nations, the unwillingness of the United States to enter the World Court, and the rise of Hitler all pointed to the possibility of another major war. In 1926 the American Friends Service Committee began a program in which students would travel in teams of two for seven to nine weeks around a relatively small geographic area. Using a second-hand car for transportation, and generally camping out at night, they would seek to arrange speaking engagements for themselves on the subject of "peace" with anyone who would listen to them.

The Y.P.R.U. had to raise around seven hundred dollars each year to sponsor a Peace Caravan. In 1930, the first year it was attempted, the effort was unsuccessful. In 1931 the idea took, however, and the first Caravans hit the road. Some of the flavor and spirit of the Caravan experience is invoked by a selection from the diary kept by John Brigham and Homer Thomas as they caravaned their way around Ohio in 1934. We reproduce it as they wrote it.

Friday - July 28 - Brite and Fair - Warm - We packed camp today, made
our final visit with our host and hostess, gorged ourselves at an
enormous dinner, and moved to Covington in the afternoon. Covington
is a progressive little town of 1800 inhabitants (600) souls). *estimate
Tonight we are in a City Park, with wading pools, horse troughs, 'n'
everything. We took a bath about 11 PM in the horse trough in order
to be sweet and clean when calling on the local highlights in the
morning.
Before going to sleep Homer and I had a long discussion on the merits
and demerits of caravaning.......
Friday July 29 - This morning we tramped the streets of Covington looking
for an honest man. Finally, we found him, a Legion man who opposed
all Communists. We talked, told him our object, convinced him we were
not Communists; so we have decked that rumour.

Also we arranged meetings at the Congregational Christian Church, the
Presbyterian Church, and the Kiwanis Club. There may be others but we
haven't found them. The Evangelistic Mission Church is engaged so we
can't lead them in fervent prayer.

In the evening, we were discovered by a family of tranocents from
California. (We are camped in a community pk. and tourist camp.)
The couple wanted to play bridge, and were feeling sad. They had
been away from Cal. three months and were dying for a game. So we
agreed and played a long rubber. It was nice for a change and made
us take our minds off peace for a bit.

Local Group Programming

I expect that the experiences undergone by individual local group
members in Y.P.R.U. and Y.P.C.U. were not very different from the experiences of local group L.R.Y.'ers. The syle of local group programming,
its degree of formality, and the nature of its content has changed considerably over the years however. It is the change in programming styles
that is most evident in reading over the archives of the two groups.

As has been previously indicated, the program efforts of the Y.P.C.U.
tended to be more devotional than those of the Y.P.R.U. in the early days.
By the 1920's however, the program prompters published by the Y.P.C.U.
national headquarters reflect a move toward more varied and secular topics.
One program booklet has program suggestions listed under the categories of
Work, Play, Thought, and Worship, among others.

Worship-oriented material remained predominant right through until the
1940's, though. The head office would also include material on Y.P.C.U.
Mission work, Biblical themes, and the odd social topic. Devotional meetings
in both groups included spirited hymn singing. Both Unions had their own

"National Hyms". The one sung by the Young People's Christian Union was entitled "Follow the Gleam":

> To the knights in the days of old
>
> Keeping watch on the mountain height
>
> Came a vision of Holy Grail
>
> And a voice throughout the waiting night—
>
> Follow, follow, follow the gleam
>
> Banners unfurled o'er all the world
>
> Follow, follow, follow the gleam
>
> Of the chalice that is the Grail.
>
> And we who would serve the King,
>
> And loyally Him obey
>
> In the consecrate silence know
>
> That the challenge still holds today.
>
> Follow, follow, follow the gleam,
>
> standards of worth o'er all the earth,
>
> Follow, follow, follow the gleam
>
> Of the light that shall bring the dawn. [5]

The Young People's Religious Union hymn was sung to the tune of "Pomp and Circumstance":

> Forward shoulder to shoulder
>
> Fling the banner of Youth
>
> On through worship and service
>
> To the glorious truth.
>
> Light of our torch wide-shining
>
> Colors always unfurled,
>
> Strength,vision, and courage
>
> We pledge to the life of the world.

Strength, vision, and courage

We pledge to the life of the world

Strength, vision, and courage

We pledge to the life of the world.

Far horizons are calling.

Here humanity cries,

Deep in the unfathomed darkness

High in the radiant skies.

Onward, questing and daring,

Mighty our chorus is hurled.

Strength, vision, and courage

We pledge to the life of the world.

Strength, vision, and courage

We pledge to the life of the world. [6]

A local group meeting which was largely devotional might include some innovations to make the service less deadly serious. For example, one group's records indicate that they used a "Train Service" where the order of service was done up like a train journey stopping at various stations.

Topic-oriented local meetings might have a single speaker, or perhaps a variety of group members contributing to discussion around a topic. Two examples of local group programs are offered below:[7]

May 25. Leader: Miss Mildred Darrah

Topic: The Coming Summer

"What I Want To Do And Why" - Mr. Jas. Walters

"What I Should Do If I Could" - Mr. Allen Carpenter

"Lessons of The Ball Park" - Mr. George Kennedy

"A Trip With the Socialists" - Mr. Watson Davis

Solo

June 8. Leader: Miss Ruth Ashley

    Topic: My Summer in a Garden

"My Maryland Farm" - The President of the Union

"Weeds" - Dr. Small

"The Inspiration of Yellow Clay" - Mr. Van Schank

Symposium: City Gardens - The Members

      Solo

The printed programs sound a little dry, but the spirit within the
locals is not far removed from that of more recent times.

Conference events also have a familiar ring. Youth conference chaos
seems to be fairly constant over time. From the Y.P.C.U. forty-fifth Annual
Meeting and Conference of October 1934 in Worcester, Massachusetts, come
minutes which convey some of the spirit of these gatherings:

A Cafeteria supper was served at 6:30 which was followed by an informal
social and dance. Bob Sproul chased around Worcester and drummed up
an orchestra when the scheduled musicians failed to appear. During
the evening Vol. 1 No. 1 of "Oooh! Scandal!"appeared. To all intents
and purposes, the paper was to be a summary of the convention doings
from day to day, but the editorship was placed in the hands of a person
with a distorted sense of humor, and he changed the intent of the
paper, making it much lighter than was intended... On Saturday morning,
due to a two inch fall of snow, the proposed picnic was cancelled and
an indoor program was substituted. Before the group broke up at the
church, Robert Barber led the 11:30 candlelight service in the church,
where he detailed some of his experiences while in the Rhode Island
Insane Asylum.[9]

The International Youth Movement

The beginnings of the international level of the liberal religious youth movement occured in the early 1920's but it was not until the Thirties that significant North American youth involvement with Europe began. This was probably a function of the personal international involvement of A.U.A. president Louis Cornish and his administration from 1927 to 1937.

The first attempt to form an international liberal religious youth organization was the Leyden International Bureau, founded in 1923. Europe, amd most particularly Germany, experienced a "youth culture" phenomenon after the close of the First World War similar to North America in the Sixties. Benjamin Zablocki quotes from a paper by a member of the Bruderhof, the most durable communal group to emerge from the German Youth Movement, describing the atmosphere of the time:

> Germany in those inflation-ridden post-war years, amid the fragments
> of Wilhelminian pomp and ambition, was a vast California of cults,
> crusades, causes, and movements. The younger generation, almost in
> a body, rejected the bourgeois ways of its elders, and hiked out into
> the country with rucksacks and short pants, a little like co-educational
> senior scouts, but with a messianic mission. This was the German Youth
> Movement.[9]

Along with the "back to nature" groups, there were national student organizations like the student Christian Movement and the Studentenschft, the latter of which called itself "a national self-governing and self-supporting student democracy."

The first representative gathering of the International Congress of Free Christians and Other Religious Liberals since the end of the First World War was held in Leyden, The Netherlands, in 1922. Dr. K.H. Roessingh of the Netherlands was appointed President of the Congress at that time. It

was he who took the initiative in organizing a youth branch of
Congress, naming it the Leyden International Bureau(L.I.B.).

For the first ten years of its existence the L.I.B. was basically a
corresponding organization centered in Utrecht. Young people within the
free religious movement in Germany organized themselves into the National
League of German Free Thinking Youth in 1924, but it was not until 1927 when
the next International Congress was held in Prague that German youth made
contact with representatives of the L.I.B.

Two small L.I.B. conferences were held in 1928 and 1929 and the Bureau
met again in 1932 in conjunction with the International Congress of 1932 in
St. Gall, Switzerland. The German group participated in the 1929 conference
and there officially joined the L.I.B. As the political tensions between
Germany and France increased in the early 1930's the free religious youth
in Germany became more involved in peace study and action. They arranged
international meeting with French youth and called them "tours of peace".
They studies the writings and the deeds of Gandhi and a group of free religious
youth succeeded in meeting him during his stay in Europe in the fall of 1931.

In 1933 all youth organizations in Germany with the exception of the
Hitler Youth were dissolved by the Nazi government. Members of the "Bund der
Freireligioesen Jugend Deutschlands" buried the flag of their group on the
grounds of their "youth home" in Mainz. It would be twelve years until the
flag could be dug up again and given to the leaders of the post-war free
religious youth.[10]

Like the North American youth organizations, the Leyden International
Bureau member groups were composed of young adults in their twenties and early
thirties. Until 1934 the correspondence work, a small publication, and the
conference organizing was all done rather informally out of Utrecht. The
newly-christened International Association for Liberal Christianity and

Religious Freedom held its 1934 congress in Copenhagen, and it was there
that the structure of today's International Religious Fellowship began to
take shape.

An international youth camp was planned to coincide with the Copenhagen
congress, and for the first time delegates from the Y.P.R.U. and the Y.P.C.U.
were in attendence.

The 1934 meeting elected an Executive Committee and created a secretariat
for the Leyden International Bureau. Annual conferences were planned. The
Swiss sponsored the first one in 1935 on the theme "Youth and the World of
Today".

The North Americans were back that year in Switzerland with an invitation
to come to Star Island the year after. The 1936 Leyden Bureau Conference
was held at Star Island in conjunction with the Y.P.R.U. convention. Two
hundred twenty young people from six countries attended. Fifty-four of
them were from Europe. It was a highly successful conference and represented
a peak of international interest among young religious liberals. However,
the promise of these events would soon be squelched by the approaching war
in Europe. The 1934 Copenhagen conference had been held in the face of
Hitler's rise to power in Germany.

The plans for re-organization laid in Copenhagen culminated finally in
1938 at Leersum, Holland, when the Leyden International Bureau was re-organized
into the International Religious Fellowship. Twenty-eight American delegares
were present at that conference. Jeff Campbell of the Y.P.C.U. was elected
the first President. Donald Harrington of the Y.P.R.U. became the editor
of the new organization's publication, Forward Together. International
Religious Fellowship (I.R.F.) was forced to become more of a dream than a
reality, however. The following year the Second World War broke out. The
I.R.F. conference of 1939 at Arcegno, Switzerland, ended only three weeks

before hostilities. Its theme was "The Demand of God to a Confused Generation".

It would be eight years from the time of its creation before the I.R.F. could have any more ongoing conferences and work camps.

"Youth Autonomy" Before the War

As the administration of A.U.A. President Louis Cornish was drawing to a close, the Y.P.R.U. enjoyed cordial relationships with the administration. The past President of the Y.P.R.U. was given an automatic seat on the Board of the A.U.A., and an A.U.A. representative usually sat in on the Y.P.R.U. Executive Meetings. The young people remained torn between their need for denominational support and contact, and their desire to remain free from denominational control. However, the Y.P.R.U. leaders from that period remember the relationship between the denomination and the youth group being one of basic trust in each other's programs and good intentions.

Of course, the age of the participants was still as much as ten years older than the age of the youth leaders of today, although the general trend as far as age remained downward. Dana Greeley was twenty-two when he was elected President of Y.P.R.U. in 1931, and Max Kapp was twenty-seven at his election that same year.

Both the Y.P.R.U. and the Y.P.C.U. remained strong within the limits of their finances and their geographic boundaries. The patterns of the past twenty years remained relatively unchanged. The Y.P.R.U., for example, still had sixty-five percent of its membership concentrated within New England and down the Atlantic Coast.

There was some fraying at the edges of these patterns, however. In 1935 as a result of an appraisal of the field work situation, the positions of field secretaries were eliminated from the program of the Y.P.R.U. All field work was henceforth to be done by subsidizing trips by the Board of Directors. This approach did not prove successful.

The stage was set for a change.

DOROTHY TILDEN SPOERL REMEMBERS GALESBURG, IL - 1920's

I was a member of the Galesburg, Illinois youth group, Universalist
Y.P.C.U. all during my high school and college days, which was the "twenties".
I think perhaps ours was an unusual group since Galesburg was the home of
Lombard College (whose charter is now the Lombard part of Meadville-Lombard)
so our Y.P.C.U. was made up of both high school and college students.

We met at the campus and walked down to the church, where we were
joined by the members coming from other directions, and, for the most part
with out adult supervision, took the meetings seriously. We tended to
follow the program suggestions of the national organization, but when they
turned out to be dull we would inevitably turn to our two favorite questions,
for debate and the arguments remained hot and heavy no matter how often it
was discussed: heredity versus environment was one of the questions; the
other, which has the greater control over human behavior, the intellect
or the emotions?

I think the reason for our long lasting success with a viable group
was the fact that we took part in the district(in those days, state)meetings
where we tried out our political wings. And a few of us managed to get to
various of the national meetings. The Illinois YPCU of those days contributed a considerable number of people to the national board, to national
offices, and to the ministry.

Perhaps another reason for our success was that high schools in those
days, at least in Illinois, did not offer a "forum" for the discussion of
wide ranging questions, and therefore anything of social or political interest
would end up in the youth group meetings.

What did we gain from it? A certain degree of facility in speaking to
sundry topics, prepared or unprepared, but not too often a push in the

direction of gaining further knowledge before continuing. A sense of
loyalty to Universalism, in part from occasional service to the church,
but more often from our excitement over the programs of the state group.
If we had a devotion in those days, it was to the cause of peace, but it
was more verbal than action largely for lack of concerted action on the
state or national level.

For most of us the high point of the year was Youth Sunday, when we
planned the entire service (once more without adult leadership since none
seemed to be forthcoming), and elected one of our number to preach the
entire sermon. It was a coveted position.

We unfortunately did not branch out to acquaintance with the Unitarians
(which would have done our souls good due to the much more liberal stance
of the Western Conference of Unitarian), though summer conferences to which we
were addicted on the state level introduced us to such Unitarian greats as
Robert Dexter and Curtis Reese.

I still hold, and am sure the others do as well, warm memories of our
gatherings at the church, despite the fact that we rarely had a group
of over fifteen or twenty. In recent years I have "chanced across" sundry
of these people as they have turned up at various meetings where I have been
on a program (some of them no longer Unitarian Universalist, some of them
still active in our Association). Always the "do you remembers" include not
only our high school and college days but our explorations of the world of
religion and social injustice done together in the Y.P.C.U.

Chapter 4:   REORGANIZATION AND READJUSTMENT

The joint slogan of the American Unitarian Association and the Young People's Religious Union during the 1920's and 1930's seemed to reflect honeymoon times. It proclaimed:

"The Spirit of Youth in the Life of the Church

Is the Hope of the World!"

Frederick May Eliot was asked to preach the Anniversary Sermon at the May Meetings of 1935 on this subject.

This ceremonial optimism was a brave show in view of a rather depressing institutional picture for the Unitarian and Universalist churches, and therefore for their youth affiliates as well. All were faced with a low ebb in membership, financial strength, and leadership.

The Impact of the Commission of Appraisal

The Unitarians were resolved to undertake a major shift in the direction of the denomination to try to reverse this tide. James Luther Adams, minister of the Unitarian Church in Wellesley Hills, Massachusetts, and Kenneth McDougall, a prominent lay member of the same church, were convinced of the need for a Commission of Appraisal to completely re-evaluate the structure and goals of the A.U.A. They dashed up and down the east coast in the spring of 1934 drumming up support for the idea, and during the May Meetings of that year, the idea became a reality.

Frederick Eliot was elected to chair the Commission. It undertook a thorough and far-reaching evaluation of the denomination. In 1936, the Commission of Appraisal published a report and recommendations which were to drastically alter the shape of the Unitarian movement.[1] The approach taken to youth programming came under close scrutiny like everything else.

From the A.U.A's point of view, a number of problems stood out.

The Y.P.R.U. was an independent affiliate of the A.U.A. which raised much
of its own money. The denomination had no direct control over it. Yet,
it was the major program related to the A.U.A. dealing with young people.
The Y.P.R.U. had always had full-time staff, consisting of an office
manager and field representatives. Given the age of the leadership (middle
twenties) and the lack of money at this time, both the A.U.A. and Y.P.R.U.
felt that this was the best that they could do. Yet, the existing organization seemed unable to cope adequately with the needs of the variety of
age groups included within the rubric "youth", particularly the college age
group.

The Commission of Appraisal's recommendations seemed to waffle on the
question of whether the A.U.A. would try to take more direct responsibility
for youth programming. However, the commission was clear about wanting to
see the program extended to become a truly national one. One the one hand,
it recommended that the A.U.A. take the position that student functions and
programming in a given area were not properly the task of the A.U.A., but
were a local and regional responsibility. On the other hand, the commission
suggested that , whatever responsibility for student programming the A.U.A.
did take on should result in close integration with the Department of
Education.

The Commission of Appraisal did approve of participation in some kind
of inter-agency directional efforts, and also recommended that young people
be given more direct recognition and responsibility within the denomination.
The Y.P.R.U. was given voting status at the annual meeting of the A.U.A.
as an affiliate organization, as well as permanent appointees to the A.U.A.
nominating committee.

In 1936, the A.U.A. appointed a special committee of five members to
consider re-organizing student work along the lines suggested by the Commission

of Appraisal. It came back early in 1937 with a suggestion for a Unitarian Student Commission to consist of eight members, four to be adults and four to be young people.

What eventually came into being in 1938 was an inter-agency group known as the Unitarian Youth Commission. The Youth Commission's focus was to be largely on the "college centers" aspect of youth programming. It had representatives of the A.U.A., the Layman's League, the Ministerial Union, the Y.P.R.U., the Universalist General Convention, and the Y.P.C.U. Stephen Fritchman was hired as Director of Youth Activities, a full-time staff position associated with this Commission.

Fritchman had received continental recognition in The Christian Register for his success with the youth group in the Unitarian church in Bangor, Maine, where he was the minister. In 1937, Frederick Eliot, as newly-elected President of the American Unitarian Association, had appointed Fritchman to be the advisor to the Young People's Religious Union. Fritchman was the first outside "professional" ever associated with the Y.P.R.U., and the first staff person ever associated with the organization who had not been hired directly by the Y.P.R.U. leadership itself. He soon won the trust of the youth leadership and the A.U.A. administration. In his advisory capacity to the Y.P.R.U., Fritchman wrote one of the best handbooks on youth programming ever put out for denominational use, Young People in the Liberal Church.

The problems within Y.P.R.U.'s organization at this time were recognized both by the denomination and by the young people themselves. The old structure was inadequate to the present or to any future needs and programs.

The Y.P.R.U. board of directors had forty-seven members, and since those outside New England could rarely attend meetings because of the costs and distances involved, the board usually met at one-third strength. The

result was that the older New England-based college students ran the
organization, in as much as board members were elected for three-year
terms and could serve as long as nine years.

Stephen Fritchman pointed to the consequences of this antiquated
structure:

> Because the Y.P.R.U. organization as at present constituted cannot
> effectively reach its membership or its potential membership in
> any helpful way of service to a degree approaching success and
> efficiency, I must report that in my observation the average church,
> even in Boston and New England, has ceased to give any deep loyalty
> or concern to the national organization. Because of a failure to
> serve its constituency the organization has lost prestige and respect.

There was not enough outreach beyond New England, and even within a
day's journey from Boston, people saw Y.P.R.U.'s procedures as undemocratic
and inadequate.

The "Committee of Four"

The Y.P.R.U.'s leadership was not totally blind to these difficulties.
However, there was particularly strong concern in the Midwest, where there
was much less regional organization than in New England in spite of a strong
base of local groups. G. Richard Kuch (pronounced "Cook") was a midwestern
Y.P.R.U.'er who was attending Meadville Theological School. In 1939 he
became involved in attempting to unite the Midwest groups in regional conferences. For sixteen years since 1923, Star Island had been the site of
the Y.P.R.U. annual meeting. There were no conferences to compare with it
outside of New England. Kuch and Paul Henniges and others organized a
conference in the summer of 1940 at Lake Geneva, Wisconsin.

As Vice-President for the Midwest, and editor of the Y.P.R.U. News respectively, Kuch and Henniges hitch-hiked and leafleted the Midwest

drumming up support for Lake Geneva, and for a stronger voice in Y.P.R.U.'s

national affairs. Regional conferences were organized at Hnausa, Manitoba,

Canada, and Ardmore, Oklahoma where Y.P.R.U.'s structural problems were

discussed. After this two year buildup of strength, Kuch was a shoo-in for

the Y.P.R.U. presidency in 1941, representing a real shift in the organization's

geographic center of gravity.

At Stephen Fritchman's urging, Y.P.R.U. also in 1941 created a Planning

and Review Commission to survey the existing organization, and to recommend

changes. The idea was based on an A.U.A. model recommended by the Commision

of Appraisal. However, the committee proved ineffective.

Finally, the Y.P.R.U. called a special board meeting for February 23-

25, 1942 at the Senexet Pines Retreat near Woodstock, Connecticut. It was

an unprecedented board meeting. Twenty-three directors showed up from as

far away as Oklahoma, Illinois, Missouri, and Eastern Canada. They stayed

together for two days.

When it was over, a "Committee of Four" had been appointed to organize

the findings and make a final recommendation for the details of a re-organ-

ization . The committee members were all from the Y.P.R.U. Executive, and

included Dick Kuch, Robert Scott, Silas Bacon, and Barbara Hildreth. Within

two weeks the Committee of Four came out with a preliminary draft of new

purposes and by-laws for the Y.P.R.U., including a name change.

The Committee's original proposal suggested the new name be "Unitarian

Youth Fellowship", but there was still some dissension in the ranks about

whether the Unitarian name should be incorporated into the group's title.

The more significant problems the Committee of Four grappled with had to

do with the undemocratic structure of the Y.P.R.U., the morass of red tape

which seemed to occupy the headquarters bureaucracy (and reinforced its

remoteness from the local groups) , and the lack of adequate field work of
any professional quality.

During that spring of 1942 the Committee of Four printed a series of
preliminary recommendations. In substance its recommendations suggested
amalgamating high school and college work under one budget, with a professional and youth staff tied in with the A.U.A. Department of Education.
Internally, they recommended a reduction in the size of the Y.P.R.U. board
and provisions for more democratic procedures in the election of officers.

American Unitarian Youth

A straw vote on the Committee of Four's recommendations took place
that spring. They were then discussed and revised at the Y.P.R.U.'s
business meetings held in conjunction with the A.U.A.'s May Meetings. At
a business meeting held at the Arlington Street Church, Boston, the re-
organization plan fell three votes short of the two-thirds majority required
for approval. Finally on October 17,1942, a special meeting of Y.P.R.U.
delegates was held at 25 Beacon Street to vote on the revised plan for
re-organization. Over one hundred delegates attended.

This body voted to change the name of the organization to "American
Unitarian Youth". The age boundaries of the group were constitutionally
set at fifteen to twenty-five years. The recommendation to bring high
school and college age work under one budget was adopted. The size of
the new A.U.Y. board was reduced to fourteen representatives designated
by regions. Each regional representative was to be conscious of the
interests of both high school and college age young people, and would
represent from one to three federations. Presiding over this new board
would be an Executive Committee of four officers, to be elected by popular
vote at biennial conventions.

In his essay covering this period of A.U.Y. history, Christopher Raible points out four important aspects of the re-organization. To begin with, the whole process took place in wartime. Many people of Y.P.R.U. age were faced with the draft, and travel was governed by a priority system. There was also little money to be had for such things as travel and institutional innovations. The fact that the A.U.Y. came into being at all under these circumstances is quite remarkable.

The move to lower and constitutionally fix the age of A.U.Y. members at a range of fifteen to twenty-five years involved a significant change in the character of the leadership of the organization. Although it was still college age people who were elected to Continental office, the age of the leaders on a regional and local level had a tendency to drop there-after. The change may also have increased the influence of the adult advisor and later the Executive Director associated with the A.U.Y.

A major policy change arising out of the 1942 re-organization was that the board members had their expenses paid to board meetings, resulting in the final elimination of the inbred New England leadership in the youth movement. American Unitarian Youth was on its way to becoming a truly continental organization.

Encouraged by the opportunity for regular representation and power in the continental organization, regional groups in the A.U.Y. began to coagulate. This was the beginning of the regionalism which was so dominant in L.R.Y. during the fifties and sixties.

Arnold Westwood took over the A.U.Y. presidency in 1943, as Dick Kuch went off to a parish ministry in Illinois. Stephen Fritchman becam Director of American Unitarian Youth under the re-organization. He now worked full-time at 25 Beacon Street. Then in January, 1943, Fritchman was appointed editor of The Christian Register, the paper having been brought under the A.U.A.'s financial umbrella. His work with A.U.Y. reverted to part-time, and would eventually be consumed in controversy after the end of the war.

The Universalist Youth Fellowship

Developments paralleling those in the Unitarian youth group were also
happening in the Young People's Christian Union of the Universalist Church.
Y.P.C.U. declined during the depression, but recovered to some extent during
the later Thirties. The Rev. Fenwick Leavitt, Y.P.C.U. president from
1939-41, reported that local unions had increased in number from ninety-
seven to a hundred thirty-four between 1934 and 1939. These were all groups
affiliated directly with the Y.P.C.U. Adding in the other youth groups
in Universalist churches that were unaffiliated brought the total to two
hundred thirty, and this was the figure Y.P.C.U. would normally give in
reporting its size. In 1939, Y.P.C.U. celebrated its fiftieth anniversary
with much fanfare. A history of the Union, compiled and written by the Rev.
Harry Adams Hersey, was published to commemorate the anniversary.

There were problems at this time that prompted little celebration,
however. The organization of the Y.P.C.U. had always leaned strongly in
the "state's rights" direction. State unions held a great deal of power
and were in competition with the national body for funds and energy. The
central Y.P.C.U. structure was a cumbersome one consisting of a large
council and an executive committee. The state unions affiliated with the
national body and paid them a blanket figure in dues each year. This was
supposed to cover about half of the Y.P.C.U.'s budget and the rest was to
come out of the Universalist General Convention's Unified Appeal. The
dues were a source of tension within the organization, for they usually
weren't enough from the national point of view and always too much in the
eyes of the state unions.

The denomination was applying pressure on the Y.P.C.U. to change its mode of operation at this time, too. The U.G.C. was aware of the internal controversies in Y.P.C.U. over finances, and was concerned about the effect this was having on programming. It was also concerned about the fact that the age range of the Y.P.C.U. had dropped and younger people were coming into positions of leadership. The denomination had no formal "Department of Young People", and wanted the Y.P.C.U.'s programming to be more closely tied in with the institutional church and its perception of the kinds of programming needed.

All of these internal and external pressures brought about a major re-organization in the Universalist youth movement at the same time as the Unitarians, between 1941 and 1942. The difference between the two plans was that the Universalist re-structuring had more to do with financial and political arrangements with the Universalist General Convention (which in 1942 was also going through a re-organization which resulted in a name change to the Universalist Church of America - U.C.A.). The Unitarian restructuring represented the beginning of a different kind of youth group that was truly continental in scope.

As with the Unitarians, the Universalist re-organization was primarily the work of a small group of leaders. Fenwick Leavitt, William Gardner, and Douglas Frazier were the architects. At the 1941 Y.P.C.U. Convention, held in Oak Park, Illinois, they proposed a number of structural changes. It was a small convention, with only forty-seven accredited delegates and sixty-two people in attendance in all. They represented only nine states and twenty-one local unions.

The delegates approved a motion to rename the organization "the Universalist Youth Fellowship" (U.Y.F.). Its age range was officially set at thirteen to twenty-five years. Direct appeals to the state unions and local groups for funds were to be stopped. Henceforth the new U.Y.F. would make use of its investment income (from investments held in trust by the U.C.A.), and would be granted the remainder of its budget out of the U.C.A. Unified Appeal.

In the first year of the Universalist Youth Fellowship's existence, Dana Klotzle was elected president, [3] and Raymond Hopkins was elected vice president. [4] Douglas Frazier was appointed by the U.C.A. as their Director of Youth Activities with part-time responsibilities for U.Y.F. The relationship of this Director to U.Y.F. was described as follows:

The Director is appointed by the U.C.A. with the approval of the corporation. The Director is the professional advisor to the cor-poration. She or he is in essence the "legal advisor or counsel" of the corporation. [5]

So the U.Y.F. gained an advisor, but at the same time it lost its full-time secretarial help through this partial integration with the U.C.A.'s Department of Education.

The U.C.A. also set up a Committee on Youth Activities consisting of two U.Y.F. representatives, one U.C.A. board member, the U.C.A. Superintendent, the Director of the Department of Education, and the Director of Youth Activities. The recommended structure of this committee, as reflected in the membership described above, was that voting adults always exceed youth, with a two-to-one ration being desirable.

Wartime Programs

The new Universalist organization and staff began on a hopeful note. A bequest of $4,400 had pulled the Y.P.C.U. out of debt for the first time in several years. So the Universalist Youth Fellowship began with a balanced budget of $6,166 for 1941-42. The leadership of U.Y.F. usually came from Tufts College. Most of them were preparing for the Universalist ministry.

When the war began, U.Y.F. saw many of its up-and-coming leaders drafted, and faced increasing problems with transportation to conferences and with money.

There were positive changes in the style and content of the programs that the new U.Y.F. published from headquarters. In 1942 a U.Y.F. handbook was published composed of separate loose-leaf booklets covering the whole spectrum of leadership training and programming for local groups. The programs suggested in this 1942 handbook remained largely worship or civic-oriented, e.g. The American Way, Understanding Ourselves, The Church and Its Faith.

Programs from the national level could not halt the decline in local and state numbers and activities due to the war however. The draft was not the only problem. Much of the spare time that young people had was mobilized to help in the war effort in one way or another. National U.Y.F. leadership and programming became mostly office functions. Student work was at a complete standstill. By 1943-44 the U.Y.F. budget had been cut nearly in half to $3,300.00.

In 1943 Ann Postma succeeded Dana Kotzle as U.Y.F. president, and the Legion of the Cross for missions underwent a revival. With a great flourish, a New Church Building Fund was inaugurated for the purpose of building a memorial church to William Wesley Cromie, a young ministerial student who had died accidentally. The goal of the fund was to be six thousand dollars. Eventually, only one thousand was raised, and it was decided in the later forties to donate the money to the Association of Universalist Women for a chapel to be built at the Elliot Joslyn Home for Diabetic Boys. Other small Legion of the Cross donations went to the International Religious Fellowship and to domestic field work.

In the fall of 1944, Douglas Frazier left the position of Director of

Youth Activities and was replaced by Roger Bosworth. During that year, the national office published an incredibly-thorough Procedures guide for U.Y.F. local groups. The guide was a collective effort of old and new U.Y.F. leadership. It provided an excellent step-by-step outline of the problems and methods involved in leadership on all levels of a youth group's operation.

The U.Y.F. and the A.U.Y. remained in close touch and co-operation with each other after their re-organizations and throughout the war. They regularly exchanged delegates to each other's conventions and board meetings. A merger of the two groups was still something under consideration and experimental moves in that direction continued to be made.

As the war came to a close, the two groups co-operated in the publishing of two small magazine-sized digests. One was focused entirely on social action and was called Youth For Action. The other was a more ambitious publication designed to be the main membership periodical for both groups. Titled The Young Liberal, it was established in 1945.

Neither organization came out of the war years in a particularly strong position. However, as the soldiers came back from Europe and the Pacific, and the younger people in A.U.Y. - U.Y.F knew peace for the first time since they were children, an attitude of hope and excitement about the future was prevalent.

PHYLLIS McKEEMAN REMEMBERS LYNN, MASS - 1938-41

It was during my high school days, 1938-41 that I was a member of the Y.P.C.U. of the First Universalist Church of Lynn, Mass.

My family was active in the smaller Universalist Church in Swampscott, the adjacent town, where I had been attending church school with years of perfect attendance. However, as is often the case in the smaller churches, I was alone in my age group; and I did live in Lynn. My school chums and their older brothers and sisters were active in the Lynn church youth group. Thus it was rather a natural development for me to join. The first year I continued to go to Swampscott Sunday mornings and to Lynn Sunday evenings for Y.P.C.U.; but they transferred all of my participation and membership to the Lynn Church.

The year 1938-39 was the 50th Anniversary of the founding of the Y.P.C.U. and its origin was in the Lynn Church. My impression of joining that fall was the experience of joy and celebration that the membership of the group had reached 50 - a goal set in recognition of the 50th anniversary. Another impressive memory is that it was my introduction to Gordon McKeeman who was president. (editorial: we married six years later and "lived happily ever after"!) Alice Harrison was our Advisor and also the Director of Religious Education of the church.

We met weekly on Sunday evening and had programs and activities carefully planned by committees. Planning was done well in advance, in detail for three month intevals, with annual events projected; sometimes topics were for a series of meetings. Each meeting had a worship service led by a member of the group and coordinated with the topic of the evening; a serious program, presentation, speaker, film, or whatever; recreation/games; refreshments. We met at the church for two hours, probably between six and

eight p.m.; and there was always "the crowd" which adjourned to someone's home for a "post-mortem". Regularly we scheduled joint events with
the youth from the Jewish Synagogue and from the black church. There was
a range of special events, other than Sunday evening meetings, and group
participation was emphasized and popular even though there were a few
"couples".

Some of the members also attended the high school class on Sunday
morning --- a part of the church school program. The class met earlier
than other age groups so that those who wished to could also attend the
church service. There was rather a typical distribution of the YPCU group,
maybe a third in the high school class, maybe a quarter or less in the church
service. Also, typical was the distribution as to those from families of
the church, and those who were attending Y.P.C.U. with friends whose own families
were of other churches or unchurched.

The Lynn Y.P.C.U. was active in the North Shore League with Y.P.C.U. groups
from the geographic area north of Boston, and in the Mass.-R. I. Y.P.C.U.
There were regularly scheduled conferences and annual events. Fall, Winter,
Spring Rallies, the October 12 mountain climb up Mt. Monadnock, occasional
dances, were all events which drew attendance from multiple groups. Summer
time always meant a week at Ferry Beach and Labor Day Weekend was a special
for the post-high school age.

Something to remember in the context of the late 1930's and early 1940's
is that while the Y.P.C.U. age range started with the high school age, the upper
range was rather open-ended. Only some of the young people went away to
college, others became employed or commuted to nearby colleges. Thus it
was often the post-high school age who were the elected top leaders of the
groups, with the high school age folk serving effective apprenticeships on

on active committees, etc. The World War II draft of young men introduced a drastic change which then began to set the upper age range for high
school. In Lynn, by 1942 we had a young adult group for the post-high
school age with mostly a female membership. A major activity was a regular
mimeographed newsletter to those away, especially in service, and meetings
were continued so as to welcome any who visited home; reunions were popular.

I know that I was serving as Secretary of the Mass. - R.I. Y.P.C.U. when I
was nineteen; and when I was twenty/twenty-one and on the national board,
I was chairman of the Junior High Committee. (The former, 1942; the latter,
1943-44. This was the early recognition of the separateness of the age
groupings. The first Junior High Camp was held in 1944 at Ferry Beach.)

I have resisted name-dropping, but we continue to be in touch with a
number of people we met through Y.P.C.U. contacts, and indeed a goodly
number have been and are prominent in U.U. affairs.

LILIA JOHNSON ARNASON REMEMBERS WINNIPEG, CANADA - early 1940's

The equivalent of L.R.Y.'ers in the Unitarian Church of Winnipeg,
Canada in the early 1940's were mostly a group of Icelanders who gathered
on Sunday evenings in the church for companionship rather than a set program. When I think back I can't remember much of what we did in the way of
program. We each gave five cents every week, and with this vast sum we
managed to buy pins for each one of us with W.U.Y. (Winnipeg Unitarian Youth)
on them. I served in many positions on the Executive, including president,
and when the young people did the service at church I gave the sermon, titled
"Youth is On The March Today". It was very philosophical and liberally
sprinkled with poetry, and could probably be used today.

My memories of A.U.Y. always go back to Hnausa Camp on Lake Winnipeg,
eighty-five miles north of Winnipeg. The week there every summer was the
highlight of the year's activities for our young people's group. What I
remember most is getting up on the last morning to watch the sunrise over
the lake, the baseball tournaments, the companionship, and getting to know
the several wonderful people who came from afar to act as our advisors. The
two that I remember particularly were Ernest Kuebler and Dick Kuch, who I
still think of with fondness. We always had a wonderful week of sun, swimming,
good food, plus some very good talks from our guests.

The highlight of my A.U.Y. days was a trip to Cleveland, Ohio to a
board meeting of A.U.Y. It was the first time any Canadians were involved,
and I represented Western Canada and Leslie McMahon of Ottawa represented
Eastern Canada. This was my first time away from home alone, and today I
am amazed my parents let me go. I had to change trains in Minneapolis and
also in Chicago, so I can understand why they worried. When in Cleveland I
stayed with some wonderful people who had asked for the Canadian girl as they

thought I might know their son-in-law stationed in with The Air Force in Vancouver (only about 1500 miles from Winnipeg!). It appalled me to discover how little Americans knew of Canada.

Dick Kuch was president and as I had met him at Hnausa I was glad to see a familiar face. I still remember how nice he was to me and how he showed me around the Field Museum in Chicago on the way home. The actual meetings in Cleveland are only a blur as they were over thirty years ago.

I have only good memories of A.U.Y., and found the experience very rewarding.

Chapter 5: INTERNATIONALISM AND THE "COLD WAR" IN A.U.Y.

The decade after the close of the Second World War was one of the most turbulent in the history of the Unitarian-Universalist youth movement. There were ideological struggles within both the A.U.Y. and the U.Y.F. and their affiliated denominations over the church's relationship to communism. There was also a redefinition of the relationships between the American Unitarian Association, the Universalist Church of America, and the two youth organizations. Climaxing these institutional changes of the late 1940's was the final move towards merger, and the creation of a new youth organization, Liberal Religious Youth.

This particular period is a complex one to describe. The relationships between the political climate of America and the events and changes within the church are difficult to separate. Two chapters are called for. One details the internationalism of the post-war youth movements, and the "cold war" politics that arose out of it. The second deals with the institutional changes of the post-war period, culminating in merger.

The World Youth Conference

Since they cover the same period of years, two chapters serve as two transparencies which may be laid one on top of the other for a more complete picture. Two transparencies cannot convey a third dimension, however, and the third dimension of this period is the international political climate after the Second World War. The Allies had liberated Europe and saved the world from Nazism. During the war, the Soviet Union had changed from a suspicious enemy of the Thirties to a friend and ally. The churches and relief agencies in America turned their concern from domestic support for the war effort to relief of the devastated countries of Europe. The church

journals and A.U.Y. - U.Y.F.'s The Young Liberal of 1945-47 are full of
appeals to feed starving Czech and Dutch people, and of photographs of
students helping to rebuild Stalingrad.

So there was a widespread international consciousness, and after all
the sacrifice of the war, a heightened awareness of the fragility and significance of democracy in the world. Shortly after the end of the war,
plans were laid for a World Youth Conference, which was to be an attempt
to bring together the youth of the world into peacetime world youth movements.

The A.U.Y. and U.Y.F. leaders of the time had passed their adolescence
in war-time, and therefore had never had the opportunity for much international contact, or travel. The last I.R.F. conference on American soil
has been in 1936. During the war, emergency committees had been created
both in England and America to continue the work and to keep I.R.F. alive.
They maintained a publication entitled "Forward", but of course, with continental European participation impossible, I.R.F. could hardly be the same.

Although not directly involved institutionally with the organization
and planning of the World Youth Conference, the A.U.Y. was indirectly connected through its affiliation with the American Youth for a Free World
(an anti-facist youth organization that Stephen Fritchman had been involved
with) and through Martha Fletcher. Fletcher, an associate director of A.U.Y.,
was Fritchman's administrative assistant and was in charge of the U.S.
Arrangements Committee for the World Youth Conference.

The conference was held in London in November, 1945. Betty Green,
now A.U.Y. president succeeding Arnold Westwood, and Ann Postma, U.Y.F.
president, attended as observers for their organizations. Betty, from
Leominster, Mass., was the youngest A.U.Y. president up until that time
and was also the first woman ever to hold the office.

More than six hundred delegates from sixty-two countries attended the
World Youth Conference. The average age of the delegates was twenty-seven.
The North American youth groups had only received notice of the conference
in July of that year, so it was dominated by larger contingents from youth
groups in socialist and communist countries.

Both Betty Green and Ann Postma travelled in Europe after the conference, including in their itinerary a trip to the Soviet Union. It
was a tremendous experience for both of them. At that time, crossing the
Atlantic meant a twenty hour plane flight or a few days on a boat. Journ-
alists were the main source of news about the state of post-war Europe.
Both Betty and Ann sent back a running commentary of articles about their
travels published in The Young Liberal. When they returned, Ann Postma
was sent on a national speaking tour by the Universalist Church to bring
the message of the world youth movement to the churches and other groups.

Innuendo and Accusation

Although there were already tensions between communist and non-communist
groups at the conference, both Green and Postma came back with extremely
favorable reports about it, and about the new world youth organization which
had been created by that conference, the World Federation of Democratic
Youth (W.F.D.Y. pronounced "Woof-dee".) At its 1946 Annual Convention at
Lake Geneva, Wisconsin, the A.U.Y. voted to affiliate with the W.F.D.Y.
The U.Y.F. followed suit later that year.

The House Committee on Un-American Activities of the United States
Congress was already at this time conducting investigations of communist
influence in American life at that time. In testimony before this committee,
the celebrated double agent Herbert Philbrick (author of I Led Three Lives)
described communist organizing among the clergy and churches in the city

of Boston. He claimed that he had not expected the testimony to become
public. When it did, the names of Stephen Fritchman and Martha Fletcher
were included among those Philbrick singled out as communist sympathizers
and organizers. In fact, he named Martha Fletcher as the head of the
communist cell to which he himself belonged.[1]

The accusation was based on flimsy evidence and innuendo, and nothing
ever came of it beyond the adverse publicity, although Fritchman was called
by the House Committee on Un-American Activities for testimony.

In the fall of 1945, Fritchman solicited Dick Kuch to return to A.U.Y.
from his parish ministry to become his Associate Director. Kuch began
work on January 1, 1946.

Under the leadership of Fritchman and Kuch in the period immediately
following the war, the A.U.Y. became more involved with institutional
sponsorship of political action. A number of A.U.Y.ers also became personally involved in these actions. On January 24,1946, national publicity was given to a picket line of clergy at the General Electric Plant in
East Boston in support of the striking union there. Stephen Fritchman,
Dick Kuch, and Betty Green were among those participating. Frederick Eliot,
the President of the A.U.A., was upset by the publicity, and called Fritchman
and Kuch on the carpet for their involvement. Critics of their actions
charged the two with leading impressionable young people into activities
they did not understand which were under the leadership or influence of
communist sympathizers.[2]

Kuch later responded to this charge in an interview with the Rev.
Philip Zwerling in September, 1971:

"We saw the picketing as simply putting good words about justice
and equality to work. It's true that I did have a hell of a hold
on the kids. I tried to use that popularity intelligently. We

never painted the picture that over there was all good and over there
was all evil..

     "..for example, Betty Green came out of a conservative environment
in Leominster, Mass., and once she'd seen the larger world, you couldn't
have kept her back from doing the things she wanted to do." [3]

The International Spirit

Dick Kuch assumed a strong role in encouraging the international
interest and spirit within the A.U.Y., and through the pages of The Young
Liberal, within the U.Y.F. as well. Stephen Fritchman was by this time
under considerable attack within the Unitarian denomination for his personal political views and his style in editing The Christian Register.

Kuch spent the summer of 1946 travelling in Europe. He sat in on
the W.F.D.Y. Council meeting in Paris, and visited the Unitarian congregation in Prague, Czechoslovakia.

Kuch also reported on the I.R.F. gathering at Flagg, near Manchester,
England which had been called together to reorganize the International
Religious Fellowship. There were no official American delegates in
attendance, but otherwise the international representation was very broad.
There were delgates representing Australia, Austria, Belgium, Czechoslovakia,
Denmark, England, Ireland, France, Germany, Holland, Hungary, and Switzerland.

The group revised the I.R.F. constitution to meet the needs of a new
era and a new generation of I.R.F.'ers. A General Secretary was elected. In
a general meeting, the delegates adopted resolutions expressing good will
toward liberal German youth, and to liberal religious prisoners of war.

This meeting was written up in The Young Liberal, and the American
groups volunteered to print the I.R.F. publication, Forward Together, as
a supplement to The Young Liberal four times a year as their contribution

to the I.R.F. Meeting in their respective 1946 conventions, both A.U.Y. and U.Y.F. voted to sponsor at least one delegate to the 1947 I.R.F. Conference in Switzerland.

Also in 1946 American Unitarian Youth accredited Jean Casson as its official delegate to another large international gathering, the International Student Congress in Prague, at which the International Union of Students was founded. In a letter to Dick Kuch, Casson described some of the political tension within the American delegation over conference issues. There was danger of the delegation splitting along ideological lines.

All this international youth activity in the post-war period moved towards a giant climax when plans were announced for a World Youth Festival to be held in Prague, Czechoslovakia, from July 20 to August 17, 1947. A number of different youth organizations, particularly the W.F.D.Y., were involved in the planning, and invitations were extended to governments and youth groups the world over. However, it was the communist and socialist countries that were doing most of the planning.

During 1946-47, the A.U.Y. made plans for a new international program of its own. For five years, while the United States was involved in the Second World War, the A.U.Y. had sponsored summer work camps in different parts of the United States and Canada. They combined public service and work with a summer holiday in an A.U.Y. conference atmosphere. The work camps had been a valuable program in maintaining and vitalizing the continental thrust of the A.U.Y. represented by the 1941 re-organization. The camps were held in New England, of course, but also at places like Hnausa, Manitoba, in Western Canada, bringing the A.U.Y. groups there in closer touch with their counterparts from other parts of the continent.

The A.U.Y. decided to sponsor a work camp in Czechoslovakia. Contact with the Czech Unitarians and government was made and the event was publicized. The summer of 1947 was to be an important summer abroad.

Fritchman Resigns

There was still a long winter to come, however, between the summers
of 1946 and 1947. Criticism of Stephen Fritchman's editorial stance in
the Christian Register was growing. Many of Fritchman's critics were as
concerned about his influence on young minds as they were concerned about
his editing. In a letter to Frederick Eliot on October 24, 1946, the
Rev. A. Powell Davies of the All Soul's Church of Washington, D.C., wrote
that the youth group of his church would henceforth be "only nominally
affiliated"[4] with the A.U.Y. as long as Fritchman remained as Director.

There was concern about Stephen Fritchman's politics and activities
among some A.U.Y.ers as well. As early as December, 1945, a letter was
published in The Christian Register from Charles M. Sherover, (an A.U.Y.er
who would later be involved in the movement to leave W.F.D.Y.) attacking:

...the apparent political line of the Register Editor who must

insist on consistently identifying the various communist groups

in foreign countries as the democratic forces, and who sees in

the foreign policy of the Soviet Union the one and only hope and

guiding star of democratic freedom and progress.[5]

Fritchman won the support of the board of directors of the American
Unitarian Association when it considered his editorship in a meeting
October 9, 1946. However, the board did not drop the case there. The
evidence against Fritchman accusing him of communist sympathies was referred
to the Director of the Department of Publications and Education instead.

In January, 1947, Stephen Fritchman offered his resignation as advisor
to American Unitarian Youth effective February 15, 1947. Frederick May
Eliot's statement to the A.U.A. board concerning the resignation implied

that Fritchman had resigned as a result of the study of the material that had been handed over to the Director of the Department of Publications and Education in October.

Fritchman himself has this to say:

The reason I resigned as a youth worker was that I was tired after eight years of a job which I had done, and felt had been completed...Also the Register had become a very demanding full-time job.[6]

The following spring Fritchman resigned as Editor of The Christian Register rather than submit his editorial copy to the A.U.A. administration for approval. He subsequently decided to take his case to the people of the denomination at the 1947 May Meetings, and withdrew the resignation. The May Meetings voted with the administration, and Stephen Fritchman left 25 Beacon Street.[7]

Fritchman had been the first professional youth worker the American Unitarian Association had hired. As such he represented the beginning of adult denominational involvement in the conduct of the Unitarian youth organization. This pattern continued until 1969. Fritchman's role in recognizing the inadequacies of the old Young People's Religious Union, and in bringing together the new American Unitarian Youth is a milestone in the history of the movement. He was lucky enough to have a cadre of very talented Y.P.R.U. and A.U.Y. leaders working with him to make the reorganization effective. His leadership and insight on the printed page and in the field made "youth work" in the American Unitarian Association not only respectable, but really possible for adults to relate to.

An International Summer

Richard Kuch stayed on as Associate Director of A.U.Y. for another

year after Fritchman's resignation, and was in effect acting director.
There was growing concern within the A.U.Y. about the direction the World
Federation of Democratic Youth was taking. A promised constitutional
convention at which some of the differences over the organization's
political stance were to be thrashed out, had yet to be held.

Kuch went to Europe in January of 1947 to meet with W.F.D.Y. and I.R.F.
officials and to further the plans for the Czech work camps. Upon his
return, he wrote the only direct reference and retort concerning the
communist scare surrounding the A.U.Y. to appear in The Young Liberal, in
the March-April, 1947, issue. In it, he described the concerns he had
heard expressed concerning the influence of communism on the young A.U.Y.ers
planning to go to Eastern Europe. Kuch's reply was that with more practical
"training in democracy" through the youth movement and within the church,
our youth would be even better prepared than they were now to justify and
defend the democratic system.

This did little to quiet the criticism, however. The Czech workcamps
project was included in the controversy. On May 27, 1947, Kuch received
a telegram from the National Committee of Free Unitarians (a lay group
which had organized against Fritchman and other "communist" influences
within the A.U.A.). The telegram protested "the intention of American
Unitarian Youth to send thirty Unitarian students to communist-dominated
Czechoslovakia for six weeks this summer for amateur brick laying which
takes three years to learn...We respectfully suggest that the total of
$4,550.00 involved be donated to relieve suffering in Great Britain, France,
and other democratic countries." [8]

The delegation that went to Europe in 1947 was led by the Reverend
Bob Zoerhide of Peterborough, New Hampshire, and David Parke, who at eight-
teen years of age had succeeded Betty Green as A.U.Y. president. The work

camp at, Hradec, Czechoslovakia was the first stop. Some twenty-seven American and eighty Czechoslovakian Unitarian youth worked together fighting the spread of a disease affecting trees in the area, mining coal, and rebuilding the village of Balaze which had been destroyed in the war.

Then a group of A.U.Y.'ers went to Prague for the World Youth Festival. It was a mammoth event, with 25,000 participants from twenty-two countries. The program included sports, concerts, displays, and other cultural events.

The total American delegation that attended the festival was weak and ill-organized. This was largely due to the fact that at the last minute the U.S. State Department denied a previously granted request for transportation for up to five hundred delegates on two C-4 transport ships.

The State Department's claim was that it could only offer that kind of support to non-political groups. Consequently such "political" groups as the Yale University basketball team couldn't make it to Prague. The Festival was therefore dominated by the large contingents from the East European countries, particularly the Soviet Union, where the definition of "youth"included people as old as thirty-five. During their week in Prague, the A.U.Y.ers performed a presentation of "Songs of America" to nearly one thousand Festival delegates in Prague.

Next followed the International Religious Fellowship conference, held at Arcegno, Switzerland from August 10 to 17, 1947. The work camp, the Festival, and the I.R.F. conference all overlapped to some extent during those three weeks. The official A.U.Y. delegates were David Parke, Carl Beck, and Wendell Lipscomb. Dick Kuch came directly from the Czech work camp to the conference and was registered as an observer.

In reporting the conference in A.U.Y. publications later on, Dick Kuch described the beginning days of the conference as a series of speeches in the morning and a series of speeches in the afternoon. The theme talks were dull and disorganized. The Americans had come from A.U.Y.'s 1947 Annual Convention at Star Island with some definite proposals for a new I.R.F. The year 1946-1947 had not gone well, and the Americans were as much to blame as anyone, for they did not manage to put out a single issue of Forward Together. The Swiss finally decided to take on the responsibility themselves. Now after a disorganized year, the conference was turning out to be a bore. A group of delegates decided to take action to remedy the situation.

The Americans joined forces with the British and recruited some of the Dutch and Czechs in writing up a proposal for the conference to form itself into a series of working commissions on the various problems of I.R.F., with time added to the conference schedule for them to meet. The Commissions proposed and adopted by the conference were on organization, program, publications, membership, and extension.

The debate and politicking in the new I.R.F. was spirited, to say the least. The delegates voted to move the unofficial I.R.F. "headquarters" from Utrecht, Holland to Prague, Czechoslovakia, in recognition of the strong Czech youth movement, and as a gesture of support and hope for the continued growth of that movement. [9] The Commission approach to doing business in I.R.F. was adopted as a permanent feature and remains to this day. The American proposal to undertake the publication of Forward Together was renewed for 1947-48 and accepted. Finally, a program of attempting to contact religious liberals from outside the Christian tradition was initiated. The issue of their participation in the I.R.F. was never completely resolved, however, and would flare into a major controversy a few years later.

There was a battle over elections when many of the assembled delegates felt that they should have the opportunity of nominating from the floor candidates other than those suggested by the Executive Committee. When the electoral dust settled, Dick Kuch had been elected president of I.R.F., succeeding Karel Haspel of Czechoslovakia.[10]

The W.F.D.Y. Controversy

The American Unitarian Youth Convention of 1947 voted to re-examine the whole question of the A.U.Y.'s affiliation with the World Federation of Democratic Youth. The committee on "Co-ordination with Other Youth Groups" was commissioned to draw up a complete report on W.F.D.Y., and the pros and cons of affiliation with it. The committee's chairman was Charles Eddis, later to become an A.U.Y. president and a Unitarian minister.

The W.F.D.Y. had never enjoyed the unanimous support of A.U.Y.'ers A strong minority had opposed affiliation with it in 1946 due to its communist participants. The political leanings of the A.U.Y.'s adult leadership, the popular internationalism of the post-war period, and the personal experience of the A.U.Y.'s youth leadership in Europe had pulled the interests of the A.U.Y. continentally towards the international youth movements that were left of center. This was not a direction that had been taken without some dissent. Now this younger group of A.U.Y. leaders were coming into positions of power.

In 1948 the "Co-ordination Committee" (as it was called for short) presented a thorough fifty-page report on the W.F.D.Y. to the American Unitarian Youth annual meeting in Stillwater, Oklahoma. The report included a history of W.F.D.Y., an analysis of the political sympathies and affiliations of the W.F.D.Y. leadership, personal observations and reports from A.U.Y.'ers at London in 1945, and at Prague in 1947, plus a fair list

of pros and cons on whether or not to discontinue affiliation. On top of
that there was also a capsule summary of the liberal and communist philo-
sophies.

A last straw for many of the A.U.Y. leaders had been the purging of
the only non-communist member of the W.F.D.Y.'s Secretariat. A.U.Y. wrote
a letter condemning the move. By the time the question finally came to
the 1948 Annual Meeting, A.U.Y., U.Y.F., and the American Youth for a
Free World were the only American affiliates W.F.D.Y. had left.

Informal discussion on the matter happened all week at the conference.
W.F.D.Y. material was on hand to read, and a pro-W.F.D.Y. film was shown.
Debate on the floor of the annual meeting lasted one and a half hours, and
at last the convention voted to disaffiliate. A committee of A.U.Y. Council
members, including Peter Raible, Leon Hopper, Kurt Hanslowe, and Louise
Gartner, was appointed to write up a statement explaining the decision.

The Universalist Youth Fellowship took the same action later that year.
Its resolution of disaffiliation declared that the action was taken because
the World Federation of Democratic Youth "has become primarily a political
propoganda organization, with which the Universalist Youth Fellowship,
being primarily a religious organization, has little in common."[10]

The W.F.D.Y. controversy within the A.U.Y. and U.Y.F. did not make
a big splash on the local level. The debate tended to be largely among
the continental and regional leaders over a two year period. The Universalist appeared to be following the Unitarian lead both in affiliating
and disaffiliating from W.F.D.Y. This was partly because their convention
was held later than the Unitarians. More significant, however, is the
fact that the Universalists did not and could not participate in all this
international activity to the same degree the Unitarians could because they

did not have the money to do it, institutionally or individually.

The furor surrounding Stephen Fritchman and the W.F.D.Y. was reflected
in the larger battle being waged in the denomination and in society at
large. The Unitarian Service Committee was caught up in a communist controversy of its own at this time, and many of the churches and denominations
were touched by the beginnings of what would develop into the witchhunts
of the McCarthy era.

The international spirit of co-operation and friendship which insti-
gated the whole controversy should not be dismissed because of the dissension
that developed from it. Valuable connections were made during that time,
most particularly with the revived International Religious Fellowship.

I.R.F. On Firm Ground

The International Religious Fellowship continued to sputter along
during the latter part of the 1940's. The year 1947-48 was nearly as
disorganized as the previous year in spite of the successful 1947 conference.
Dick Kuch simply could not put as much effort in as was required to main-
tain a strong I.R.F. throughout the year, and when he resigned from the
A.U.Y. staff in mid-year, it was too late to find anyone else who could
carry the ball. Forward Together was not printed by the Americans for the
second year in a row. On top of that, the new communist government of
Czechoslovakia greatly tightened its travel restrictions for Czechs, and
for foreigners. The I.R.F. Secretariat in Czechoslovakia could not function. Halfway through the year, it became apparent that the 1948 I.R.F.
Conference could not be held in Czechoslovakia as planned.

The site was changed to Denmark, but the conference finally drew
only ten people from outside of Denmark. The heretofore strong Czech group
was unable to get passports. Lawrence Jaffa and Charles Eddis attended

from America. Eddis had been designated as the A.U.Y.'s official international delegate, and spent that summer going to the conferences of
A.U.Y.'s remaining international affiliates.

The I.R.F. ceremonially elected Ludek Benes, a Czech, as the new
president, but major responsibility for 1948-49 was to rest in the Executive Secretary, Brian Whitehead of England. Plans were laid for the 1949
conference to be held in Holland in conjunction with the International
Association for Religious Freedom congress.

Eddis took his I.R.F. responsibilities seriously over the following
year. He took over the editorship of Forward Together, and turned out
good issues on time. An American I.R.F. Committee was formed with A.U.Y.
and U.Y.F. representatives, and in 1949 four A.U.Y.ers were able to travel
to Holland. With an annual budget of about three thousand dollars and a
stronger leadership core, I.R.F. grew steadily stronger after 1949, achiev-
ing the continuity and stability necessary to hold together an organization
so spread out.

The international enthusiasm within our youth movement during the
post-war period really made it possible for the International Religious
Fellowship to transcend its European base, and complete the process of
including the North Americans within their fold, a process which had only
begun when interrupted by the Second World War.

ROBERT H. Mac PHERSON REMEMBERS WEST SOMERVILLE, MASS - 1940 - 1943

Thirty five years ago there were weekly Sunday night meetings of
young people, ranging in age from fourteen to twenty, at the West Somerville Universalist Church, West Somerville, Massachusetts. Programs often
featured a guest speaker; a discussion about the next picnic; plans for
a roller skating party; gathering together to attend the Middlesex League
of the Universalist Youth Fellowship; a special visit to a Universalist
Church beyond the area of the afore-said Middlesex League; a ten minute
devotional service led by one of the members; plans for a Youth Sunday
program to be presented at the Sunday morning worship; songs around the
piano, sacred, secular and "pop;" game periods featuring items found in
most recreational handbooks, similar to those we had learned at girl scouts
or boy scouts; perhaps a pancake supper prepared by parents and/or, and
especially, the minister.

One of our ministers was very strong on the Conscientious Objector
Movement and brought in theologue friends from neighboring Tufts College
(not yet a university) to explain why Conscientious Objectors were doing
more to defend their country than those who bore arms. This minister also
laughed easily and his young wife seemed to enjoy the onslaught of loud
teenagers at their tiny apartment as well as at the church meetings. He
was run out of the church by the ruling elders for preaching sermons against
war.

The next minister was a little older, thirty-four, the father of three
and bearing other marks of bourgeois respectability. He turned out to be
only a little less radical in his social ideas, but knew how to clothe his
more violent sentiments in self-deprecation and obscurantism.

A few of the items discussed overtly by the members before, during

and after meetings included: How late did you stay out Saturday night?
How tiring it is to be up until two o'clock after the movies and a visit
to the dairy bar, and a few kisses on someone's front porch, and then
have to revive on Sunday morning to attend Sunday School. Whether it
is more funny to drop a button into the U.Y.F. offering plate, together
with your nickel donation, or a metal slug. Why does Susie, presumably
out of earshot on the other side of the room, suddenly seem to be dress-
ing herself like a movie starlet when she dosn't have the figure for that
kind of thing and just looks silly with four inches of makeup? Whether
smoking is a good idea. Some of the most avid smokers thought it was
fun to blow smoke through a handkerchief, leaving a nicotine stain. Whether
we should take the Bible as seriously as our Baptist friends do, and whether
they really take it seriously, and how smart we are to be able to dance in
church, and how unfortunate the Methodists are that they can't, and whether
it is bad to drop a copy of the Bible on the floor, and why do Catholics
believe in having so many children, and if so how come some of our Catholic
friends are in one, two or three children families?

One night when one of the Conscientious Objector theologues, from
Crane Theological School at Tufts, came to our meeting, the question of
the hour was whether fighting the Germans was similar to protecting our
neighborhood and the virtue of neighborhood women from a maniacal gunman.
Opinions were heated, but the Patriots were worsted by the Pacifists. The
discussion continued on the walk home, but here the Patriots got the upper
hand, and without violence. Most of the boys, who outnumbered the girls by
two to one in this youth fellowship, were drafted or enlisted within a year
following Pearl Harbor.

One Sunday night there was a well attended forum, with adults invited.
Two young people, a minister and a parent, made five minute statements on

the topic, "Parents and Children Should Understand One Another." A lively discussion ensued. One of the parents in the audience titilated everyone, of all ages, by saying that he thought kissing was a wonderful form of exercise and that he wanted, "All he could get until I die!" He died not more than a decade later of heart disease, complicated by a World War I pulmonary injury that had been inflicted by chlorine gas.

The members of this Universalist unit gave at least cursory attention to race relations; an historical view of the Bible; the need for world understanding, the uncertainty of immortality; the small likelihood of personal immortality; the enduring values of Judaism and Christianity; and the desirability of securing a good education. Temperance lectures were still being offered in Sunday School in the West Somerville Universalist Church as late as 1940. A new generation of enlightened, liberal Universalist ministers displayed a generous degree of sobriety but did not seem to think the issue of alcohol worthy of consideration. Sex education was hinted at but discussed in only the most oblique terms. The boys and girls discussed these affairs privately, and sometimes even in mixed groups, but restraints were present.

For example, the youthful, dashing president of Tufts College advised the members one night that kissing on the first date might be a little abrupt, but could be countenanced if not conducted with wild abandon.

The gathering of war clouds before and after Pearl Harbor produced a clear sense that all was not right in the world. Still, even the shock of Pearl Harbor did not diminish a sense that anything Americans wanted was right. Having struggled out of the Great Depression, America could do probably what it wanted to do.

Attendance at the Universalist Youth Fellowship in this congregation of less than a hundred families ranged from four to twenty youths out of

95

a total of twenty-five members. At least six were drawn into the program because of friendship. Two or three joined the church and took part in other phases of church life at a later date. Most of the members were unaware that their circle was considered an optimal number for an adolescent group by nonsectarian youth educators, and considered their group, like the church, to be "small." They appeared to consider smallness to be linked with their own commonsensical, naturalistic views of religion, brotherhood, the cosmos and other topics. Sometimes it was stated as being unfortunate that larger churches, Protestant and Catholic alike, were so hidebound, dogmatic, sealed from reality and obsessed with such rituals as "giving up for Lent" and eating fish or not eating pork. On the other hand, some members seemed to think it might not be a bad idea to try giving up something that one liked during Lent just to see if it could be done.

So, what does it all add up to? The Sunday night meetings which were so central and time consuming for a brief, intense time of growing up might seem to have vanished. For one of the members, these adolescent evenings still cast a spell. They offered a chance to socialize. They also encouraged the sharing of ideas not readily discussed in the public school, sorority, fraternity or other matrices. The meetings were a valid excuse to parents, if not teachers, to postpone high school homework. There was aesthetic stimulation through poetry, music and non-popish candles lit sometimes in a youth-led vesper service which were described as "this little liberal light of mine." To some of the members, these meetings were an escape from the authority of home, and school. To others they may have symbolized a contact with some kind of ideal for living. To all, they were an opportunity to celebrate the fact of being young.. The youthful, emerging confidence.

Two of the twenty four have offered, as this item is written, a total of forty three years of professional leadership to a total of eight Unitarian and Universalist churches. One served as board member to the Universalist Publishing House. Another married a researcher into programmed education and moved to California. Another has served on the official boards of two New England churches. If what one recalls of a third of these twenty five may be representative of the whole, this tiny assemblage of youth and energy may still be unfolding, nurturing, producing.

How much of this nostalgic recollection has any relationship with what really went on in 1940-1943? This observer will likely never be sure. Only consider a poem which we used to sing to a mawkish melody. Maybe the reader will find a connection with the events described. Maybe not! However, we did sing it quite often and these lines are penned from memory

> "That cause can neither be lost nor stayed,
> which takes the course of what God has made,
> And is not trusting walls and towers,
> But slowly grows from seed to flowers.
>
> Thereby itself like a tree it shows,
> That high it reaches as deep it grows,
> And if the tree by the storm is shattered,
> What then if thousands of seeds it scatters."

                    (Source forgotten, but words remembered.)

LORNA DAVIDSON REMEMBERS I.R.F. IN EUROPE - 1939-46

Until 1939 the I.R.F. was organized only through its headquarters
in Holland, which kept in touch with the Youth Groups of the churches
which were members of the I.A.R.F. Thus, in England, the F.O.Y. and
the Y.P.L. and a few individual members were in contact with Holland,
but there was no English I.R.F. committee. In 1940, after the invasion
of Holland, Elspeth Hall (now Rev. E. Vallance) was mainly responsible
for suggesting the setting up of an Emergency Committee in England to
keep in touch with members in countries still free from Fascist domination.
Joan Hartley (now Mrs. J. Haenisch, and living in California) undertook
the enormous task of Contact Secretary. Our chief aim was to keep the
Fellowship alive until it could function, as before, as an international
body. To keep the I.R.F. going here we organized week-end conferences,
produced duplicated issues of an English language 'Forward Together' and
spent many hours preparing an ambitious 'Study Guide'. We exchanged
letters with members in America and were glad to hear that their activities
increased as the Unitarian and Universalist Youth Groups worked more closely
together.

When I became Secretary I was handed a strong cardboard box, containing
many small slips of thin paper with names and addresses of the members of
the various national groups known to the Dutch at the outbreak of the war.
I was told that if the Germans invaded Great Britain the lists must be
destroyed, as it would be dangerous to have international sympathies
during a Nazi occupation. At Christmas 1944, when I was away on a visit,
a 'flying bomb' landed on the house in Oldham, Lancs. where I had 'digs'
and completely demolished it. Apparently, it went through my bedroom,
and if I had been there then I would not be here now! My landlady was

badly injured and some of our neighbours killed. It was some days before
I heard what had happened and returned to claim my possessions. The stuff
that had been pulled out of the wreckage of several houses - furniture,
clothes, curtains, carpets, cases, books, papers - wet and, sometimes,
blood-stained - was piled up in dusty heaps in an old Sunday School, and
friends helped me to rummage through it and to find what was mine. I
found a few odd shoes, a case of clothing, some of my books but I realized
that what really matters is contacts. Clothes I could make or borrow,
furniture replace, shoes were a problem at that stage of the war and books
difficult - but the thing that I must find was that list! At last someone
popped up from behind a torn settee and held up the box, unopened and
safe. "Is this what you are looking for?" That list was, in fact, our
chief means of re-establishing communications after the war.

In the summer of 1945, when first Holland and then the rest of Europe
was gradually and painfully freed, we began to receive and send letters
and to hear of all that had been endured. We sent a letter to everyone
on that list asking for information and spent all our spare time and much
of the nights in replies. The people of Holland and expecially those in
the Arnhem area were destitute. They were literally starving, having had
only small and irregular rations during the occupation, and been robbed
even of the bicycles on which they at first travelled long distances to
buy food from the farms. Their houses were often ransacked by the German
soldiers. Their young men had lived in hiding to avoid forced labour in
Germany; many had been in concentration camps, and very many were ill.
And yet the strange thing is that some of the Germans still believed that
they were welcomed in Holland. We had a fine German Quaker Esperantist
member in the Camp in Leersum, Holland, in 1938. He had refused military

service (brave man!) and had joined the Red Cross. When he was sent to
Holland he wrote to an I.R.F. member, who was also an Esperantist to invite
her to meet him. She was in a dilemma. Imagine what the Dutch would think
of a girl who fraternised with a German! Nevertheless, she went - and
found that he had no idea of the feeling that the invasion had aroused
in Holland. I imagine that the meeting was brief, but at least it shows
that the spirit of our fellowship could pass over even that barrier.

The greatest joy in that year was to hear from the Secretary of
the I.R.F., Jeltje Vorster, and to start planning for the revival of the
Fellowship internationally. We joined in a scheme to send Red Cross parcels
of necessities to Dutch people in need and, optimistic as ever, we organized an 'International' conference at Flagg for the summer of 1945, but
we could not persuade the authorities to give visas to visitors from
abroad. In the December we issued the first post-war printed 'Forward
Together'.

Finally, in the summer of 1946 (in the week in which bread rationing
started in Britian) we managed, with the help of that General Assembly,
to hold a week's conference in Manchester, attended by several of our
old and some new friends from Czechoslovakia, Holland, Denmark, Belgium,
Switzerland, Austria, France, and Eire. It was the most exciting week of
my life! And now 'old' was the relevent word - for most of us had passed
the magic age of 35 and we had to hand on the Fellowship to the younger
ones. For me, the war really came to an end that week - but not the
friendships we had formed. For we have carried them on into the I.A.R.F.
There, we do not meet so often and our numbers are growing less - but we
have shared an experience which goes very deep and it has coloured our
outlook ever since, for to quote from one of the first letters we received

from Holland 'it was a real help to know that there was in this dreadful time a fellowship, the members of which could not reach one another but who had the same belief and who - as we - certainly would re-live the splendid hours we were together, working, talking, singing and praying. Though separated, we felt bound together with them.'

The first Executive Committee of Y.P.C.U. (1889-90).Note - Three Women!

The Y.P.C.U. Convention of 1895 Unity Church (Unitarian) in Boston,
600 delegates attended - the largest Y.P.C.U. convention ever.

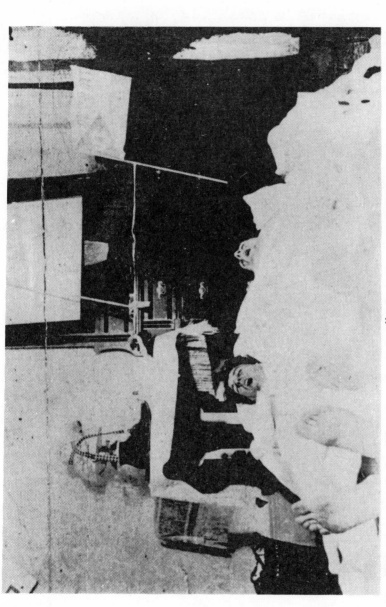

This photo was originally captioned: "Some young people at a convention – on a hot night!" Detroit Y.P.C.U. Convention:1897.

From left: Harold Canfield, Y.P.C.U. National Secretary; Elmer Felt, a Y.P.C.U. President; Harry Fowler, another Y.P.C.U. President. (Photo taken about 1900)

The Y.P.C.U. Executive 1903-05 From left, Back, H. Ida Curry, George F. Sears, Rev. John John Murray Atwood, Elizabeth W. Bacon Front, Seated Harry Adams Hersey, Louis Anim Ames, Chtham W. Pierce

Y.P.C.U. members "riding the rails" between LaCrosse, Wisconsin and St. Paul, Minnesota for a convention: 1909.

Returning by steamer down the St. Lawrence river
from - 1906 Detroit, M.I. Y.P.C.U. convention

(H. Kirk photo
H.D.S. library)

Moc**K** wedding on excursion after the 1908
Y.P.C.U. convention in Washington D.C.

(H. Kirk photo,
H.D.S. library)

Automobile sight-seeing trip at 1909 Y.P.C.U. convention in Minneapolis/St. Paul
(H. Kirk photo, H.D.S. library)

Couple at 1908 Y.P.C.U. convention in Washington, D.C.

(H. Kirk photo, H.D.S. library)

A page from Onward celebrating the dedication of the Shinn Memorial Church in Chattanooga, 1917. The church was built with support from Y.P.C.O.

MISSIONARY PILGRIMAGE of the YOUNG PEOPLE'S CHRISTIAN UNION of the UNIVERSALIST CHURCH, TO ITS TWENTY-NINTH ANNUAL CONVENTION and the DEDICATION of the HINN MEMORIAL CHURCH AT CHATTANOOGA, TENN., JLY 8-22, 1917.

OUILLEN HAMILTON SHINN, D. D.

Dr. Shinn was the ·atest missionary of · Universalist Church. e founded more than .y Churches and many unday Schools and nions; erected thirty- e church edifices, and nt twenty-nine men to the Ministry.

✳ ✳ ✳

In connection with the onvention an Evangel-istic Campaign will be conducted under the auspices of the Young People's Christian Union. Evangelists will visit many of our Churches in the Southland. Special meetings are also being planned in places where there are no Universalist Churches. Any minister who wants to be a missionary for a few days should send his name at once to Mr. Manning.

If you want to have Universalism preached in your town next summer communicate with Rev. Stanley Manning, 2518 First Avenue S., Minneapolis, Minn.

Dana Greeley and Deborah Webster
"Doing the Varsity Drag"
at the Shoals 1926

The scenes from The Free Religious Youth Conference in
1934 where I.R.F. was organized

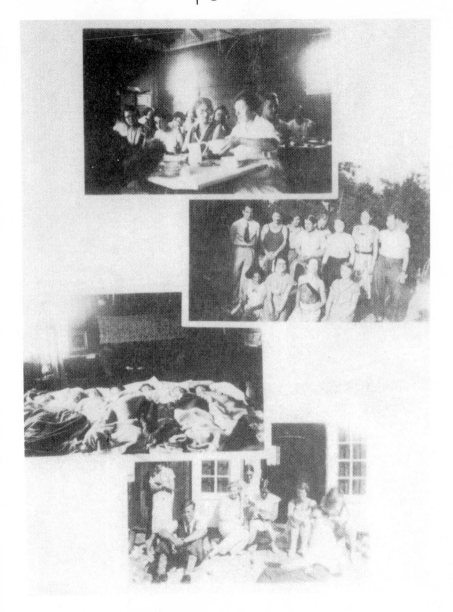

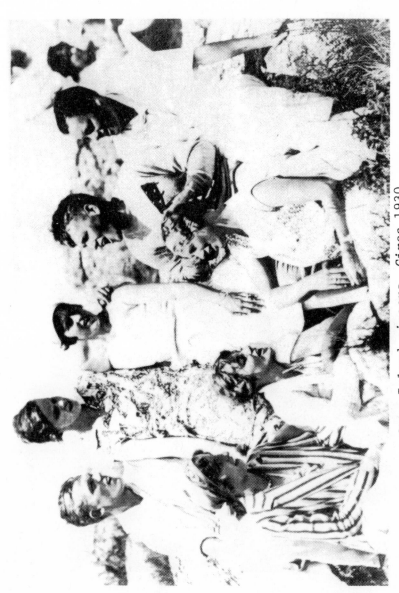

Star Island singers, Circa 1930

Y.P.R.U. at the Shoals 1928. Can you identify Bill Rice? Dana or ~~Denny~~ Greeley? Ruth Twiss?

The "Young People's Staff" at A.U.A. headquarters 1941
L to R Dorothy Nugent, Elizabeth Hunter, the Rev. Stephen Fritchman, Constantine Cone

Delegates vote to create American Unitarian Youth October 17, 1942 Chapel at A.U.A. Headquarters.

Dick Kuch tallies votes for new home of Unitarian youth organization. October 17, 1942.

Harold Shelley helps Dick Kuch load up the famous
hudson (1942)

A summer conference workshop at Hnausa, Manitoba, Canada in 1941. Summer A.U.Y. Conferences outside New England were a new thing at the time.
From Left: Philip Petursson Jr., Thora Asgeirson, Dick Kuch, Mrs. Johnson, Joan Jonasson, Lilia Johnson

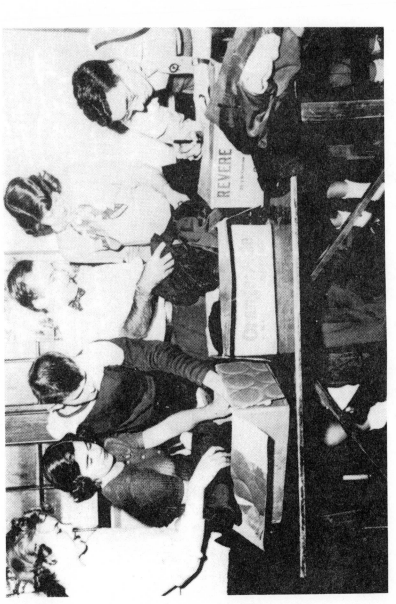

U.Y.F. & A.U.Y. members pack clothing for post-war relief packages to Europe 1946.

A.U.Y. domestic
work camp in Dallas,
Texas 1946
Center: Chris Raible

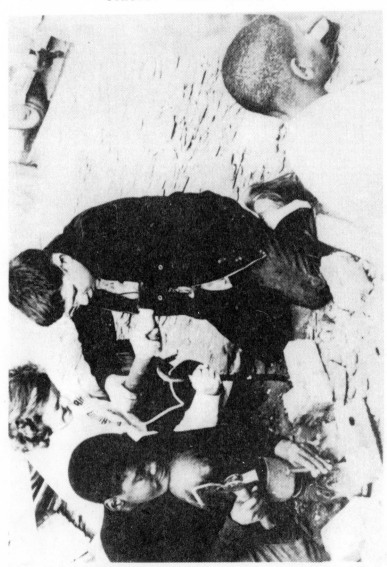

A.U.Y.'ers on the way to a Czech
work camp.   1947

David Parke and Betty Green hold up a
"Czechslovakian Unitarian Youth" T-shirt
   1947

The 1948 A.U.Y. Continental Convention Stillwater, Oklahoma The first West of the Mississippi or south of the Mason- Dixon Line.

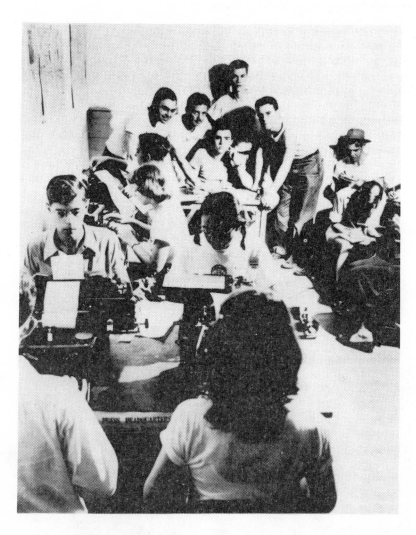

The Press Room A.U.Y. Continental Convention 1948 Stillwater, Oklahoma

The A.U.Y. Council at Hinsdale, Il. December 1947
From left: Chuck Eddis, Peter Raible, Carl Beck, Nan Reese, Leon Hopper.
Next two unknown.

The barriers to merger come tumbling down. Rozelle Royall and Leon Hopper pose for dramatic photos at Lake Winnepesaukee, June 1951.

U.Y.F. Officers 1951-52 at the Uni-Uni Conference Lake Winnepesaukee, June 1951. Front (from left): Rozelle Royall, Richard Woodman, Marilyn Moore, George Ulrich Rear: Fannie Engstrong, Dick Dringon

The 1953 Joint A.U.Y.-U.Y.F. Convention that finally voted to creat: L.R.Y.

Signing the L.R.Y.'s Corporate papers, Dec. 16, 1953
L. to R. Ralph Graner, Secretary A.U.Y., Lorraine Savage, Secretary U.Y.F.
Alma Harrison, Director of Youth Activities, U.C.A., Sam Wright Director A.U.Y.
Clara Mayo, President A.U.Y. James Monroe Jr., V.P., U.Y.F. Eileen Layton, Assoc. Director
                                                                              A.U.Y.

"May I have this Dance?"
New England — New York U.Y.F. Rally 1953   credit John A. Bachman

The First Corporation (Board of Trustees) of L.R.Y.- December 1953
President Clara Mayo front center.

German Free Religious Youth on a *outing near* Czech town with Unitarian Young People's League of England, 1951. This was their first contact since the war. John Quirk is left in the white shirt. Keith Treacher is holding the flag.

The I.R.F. Executive Committee meeting at Offenbach 1956.

Official I.R.F. Ceremony at F.O.Y. house in Flagg, England 1951. Keith Treacher is presented with a Free Religious Youth pendant. Ron McGraw shyly lowers his head. Deither Gehrmann is at right.

"No, I don't understand them either."
Mary Vann Wilkins and Maria Fleming (1st two presidents of L.R.Y.) examine
L.R.Y. By-laws U.U.A. President Dana Greeley and L.R.Y. Executive Director
Leon Hopper. December 1961)

The organizational conference of Student Religious Liberals·Lake Forest College, ~~Ela~~. 1961

I.R.F. - S.R.L. Joint conference Springfield, Mass. 1962

Rev. Orloff Miller & S.R.L. ... Europeans study trip in Luxemburg /
(Mid-sixties.)

photo
credit: Charles Flagg

I.R.F.'ers reach new heights
One of many post-war I.R.F. conferences in Switzerland.

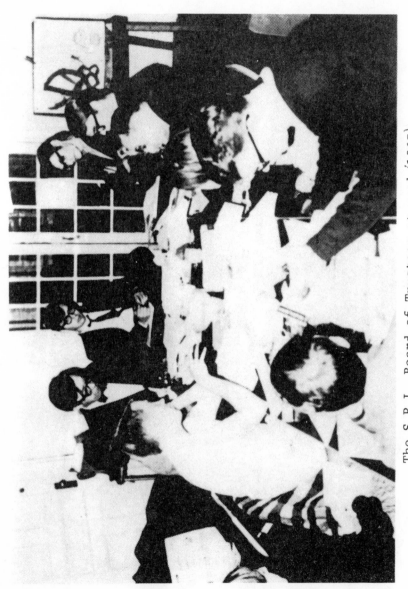

The S.R.L. Board of Trustees at work (1967)

L.R.Y. Field Directors Marsh Agobert and Peter Hankin puzzling over a turn of phrase in the "Youth Agenda" (April 1969).

The Youth Caucus "occupying" the Statler Hilton mezzanine at the 1969 General Assembly.

The 1970 Continental Conference Committee, creators of the first
a - thematic Continental, <u>Stewed Rhubarb</u>. From top (left to right)
Jon Tilson, Bob Salisbury, Peedie Parks, Wayne Arnason, Erica Gerson,
Dave Shay, unknown, Foster Channock.

The ingredients in Stewed Rhubarb: The 1970 Continental Conference Seabeck, Washington

The 1974 L.R.Y. Board of Trustees "Last Day of Boards"

"We flip for L.R.Y." Executive members Holly Horn and Gale Pingel
make a pancake breakfast for the U.U.A. Board January 1973

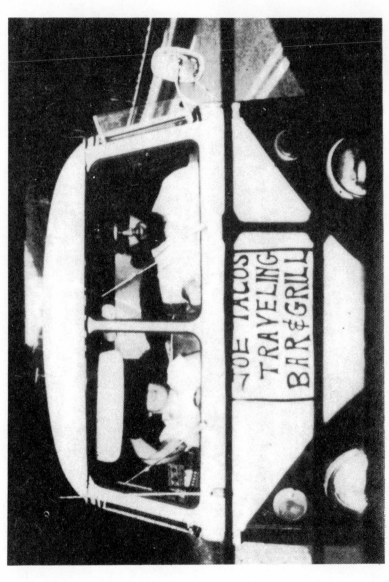

The eternal L.R.Y.'er, Joe Taco (David Knight in this case), at the wheel on the endless L.R.Y. field trip.

A familiar scene at General Assemblies in the 70's. U.U.A. Board member Frank Robertson and L.R.Y. Director Nada Velimirovic speak to the issue of L.R.Y. Funding. Brian Oelberg at left.

"International Contacts." I.R.F.'ers Debby Bright, Sherry Neiderer-Scherrer, Roger Smart, Alicia Bright and Chris Groncha waiting for the ferry to Holland. (1979)

"Re-inventing the wheel".....

Chapter 6: WE WOULD BE ONE

A very dynamic group of youth leaders in the post-war era, and not
just the domestic and international politics of the time, make this a
significant period in this history. Many of the young people involved
in the youth movement leadership at this time went on to enter the ministry and continue to serve Unitarian Universalist parishes. Their
initiative and continuing work during this period brought the U-U movement through the institutional changes which resulted in the creation of
the Liberal Religious Youth.

The Hinsdale Meeting and its Aftermath

People make the politics, and the leaders of the American Unitarian
Youth in the late forties were a highly political group. David Parke
succeeded Betty Green to the A.U.Y. presidency in June 1947 after coming
up through the Executive Committee ranks for three years. Park was a
freshman at Antioch at the time, and took the year 1947-48 off from college
to work full-time for the A.U.Y.

His vice-president was Charles Sherover. Sherover and Peter Raible
had organized the Chicago Area Council of Liberal Religious Youth in January,
1947, and represented a major center of influence in A.U.Y. west of Boston.

In his essay, "A Short Subjective History of the Unitarian and Universalist Youth Movements", Leon Hopper has pointed to organizational changes
in December, 1947, as constituting a milestone on the road to the formation
of Liberal Religious Youth. He emphasized the new relationship with the
denomination that arose from this meeting, particularly in terms of how
it promoted the idea of "youth autonomy" within A.U.Y. and later L.R.Y.

Hopper described the meeting as follows:

The present and future shape of L.R.Y. and of the Continental as we know it today was cast in a meeting in Hinsdale, Illinois, in December, 1947. Ernest Kuebler, Director of the A.U.A. Department of Education, and Dr. Frederick May Eliot, President of the A.U.A., met with the American Unitarian Youth Council to discuss the future relationship of the A.U.Y. to the A.U.A., and that of A.U.Y.'s professional staff to the Association.

The A.U.A. staff proposed a plan to the A.U.Y. Council: the Department of Education to hire a Director of Youth Activities to be paid by the Association and the A.U.Y. to hire and pay for its own staff from its own budget. (The A.U.Y. received funds from the United Unitarian Appeal.) The Council presented many reasons for rejecting this proposal, but in the end accepted it. And this was the beginning of "youth autonomy".

The picture Hopper presents is one of A.U.A. pushing the A.U.Y. into a more autonomous position, almost against the latter's will. This is true to a certain extent. Stephen Fritchman had resigned as A.U.Y.'s adult Advisor in January of 1947. Dick Kuch was the senior staff person of A.U.Y. in 1947, and by the end of the year his resignation seemed imminent, although not yet announced. Controversy had continued to surround A.U.Y.'s 1947 summer activities, both in Europe and in connection with the Star Island conference and Annual Meeting.

In its October, 1947, report, the A.U.A.'s Commission on Planning and Review expressed satisfaction at the intensified "national activities" within the youth movement, but had certain reservations as well:

Despite these commendable activities, summer institutes have not presented the various points of view representing the Unitarian outlook; there has often not been the accompanying development of the national program has too often been lacking on the part of large numbers of Unitarian adults because of lack of information.[1]

When the A.U.Y. Council met at Hinsdale, they were faced with "Eliot and Kuebler and the boys all present explaining to us how it was going to be."[2] How it was going to be was as Hopper described it: the A.U.A. would hire and pay for one staff person, a Director of Youth Education, who would function in the same staff capacity as Fritchman and Kuch. As noted above, Fritchman was the first staff person the organization ever had who was hired by the A.U.A. All the Y.P.R.U. staff persons were responsible only to the Y.P.R.U. board, so their "autonomy" was an established fact. Although paid by the A.U.A., Fritchman had been hired in close consultation with Y.P.R.U. leaders, and of course, Kuch had come out of the ranks. The main problem with the A.U.A.'s proposal at this Hinsdale meeting was that Frederick Eliot had already decided on the person he wanted to appoint to this new staff position that he was creating, without any official prior consultation with the A.U.Y.

The A.U.Y. leaders reacted strongly against the idea of having a new staff person imposed upon them in this way, but Eliot would not budge. The result was that the A.U.Y. decided to hire its own staff people and pay for them out of its own budget, above and beyond the A.U.A.'s staff person. By February, 1948, a full-scale search for a new A.U.Y. Director was under way.

When the dust cleared in the summer of 1948, Clifton Hoffman, Eliot's choice, was on the A.U.A's staff as Director of Youth Education, with a job description having a far wider scope than A.U.Y. Hoffman was a minister who had been dean of students at the University of Chicago's Divinity School. The A.U.Y. had hired Paul Henniges, who was the minister in the Unitarian

Church in Long Beach, California. Henniges had been editor of The
Y.P.R.U. News and a friend of Kuch's during the re-organization days.
Outside of the youth leaders, the continuity in the A.U.Y. office was
maintained by Mildred Saunders (now Vickers), who as office secretary
was a mainstay of stability and efficiency in the A.U.Y.'s organization.

So the A.U.Y.'s new relationship of "autonomy" from the A.U.A. was
a mixed blessing. Financially, it was a real problem. After only two years,
the A.U.A. had to discontinue Hoffman's job due to lack of funds. In
February, 1950, Charles Eddis summarized the consequences of the new relationship:

> Two years ago A.U.Y.'s net budget was a bit over fifteen thousand
> dollars. Today A.U.Y. has approximately the same budget, but
> there is one big difference. While two years ago the A.U.A. supp-
> lied the A.U.Y. with a full-time staff of three, today A.U.Y. pays
> the salaries of its staff out of its own budget, thus reducing
> A.U.Y.'s effective budget considerably. The A.U.Y. staff has been
> reduced, and the A.U.A. staff in the youth field wiped out comp-
> letely, with the absence of a Director of Youth Education and
> of secretarial staff under him.[4]

Then, in May of 1950, the United Unitarian Appeal reached only 55%
of its goal. Everyone suffered as a result. The A.U.Y. received only
$8,312.00 out of its anticipated allocation of $14,000.00. The organization had been functioning on a hand-to-mouth basis for some years at
this point already. Money was borrowed each year in the hope that the
United Appeal would come in with a little bit extra in May, and, of course,
it never did. Beginning in 1948, Parke and Kuch had investigated the
possibility of using endowment fund capital to regain financial stability.
In 1949, the A.U.Y. annual meeting voted to remove $14,880.00 from endow-

ment fund capital to meet past debts and present expenses. Given these
circumstances, it was decided to live within the limits of a $10,814.96
budget for 1950-51. A full three quarters of that budget went into staff
salaries and office expenses. Midwinter Council Meetings had to be cancelled,
and the A.U.Y.'s continental publication, The Young Liberal, was discontinued.

Success and Failure in College Age Programming

Most of the programming that the liberal churches directed at college
age people before the Second World War happened at the local and regional
levels, under the direction of such groups as the Boston Student Committee
and individual college center ministers. The last systematic effort at
college work on a large scale was the Student Federation of Religious Liberals
back in the Twenties. The A.U.Y. had a "Student Work" Committee which
functioned on a small scale.

When the war ended, however, there was a pressing need for something
more to be done in this area. The reorganization had lowered the age of
the leadership in both the A.U.Y. and the U.Y.F. The continental leaders
were now in their late teens or early twenties and usually in their early
college years, while the age range of the local groups had lowered pro-
portionately. The young people returning from military service found
themselves older than the existing local group members, but still interested in the kind of program and group experience that A.U.Y. and U.Y.F.
provided.

The A.U.Y. Student Work Committee did some basic organizing work in
contacting students on campus, and Stephen Fritchman devoted half of his
A.U.Y. time to college work. It became apparent that there were some
strong local centers such as Berkeley, California; Chicago, Illinois;

Urbana, Illinois; and Northampton, Massachusetts where college age seminars and conferences could be successful.

At the instigation of the A.U.Y. Executive Committee and staff, a Channing Foundation was created at the 1947 A.U.Y. Conference at Star Island to serve the needs of college age people. A budge of eleven hundred dollars was granted, and a seven-person Channing Foundation Committee was set up in the Midwest to try to co-ordinate a national program using the regional committees as bases. The following summer the Universalist Youth Fellowship formalized its student work under the title of the Murry Foundation. Only a hundred dollars was allocated for their expenses, so it appears that correspondence was to be their major organizing tool. The two groups got together to publish a joint college age magazine, The Liberal's Challenge.

Organizationally neither program ever really got off the ground. Many people put a great deal of time into the effort, including the older A.U.Y. leaders such as Green, Sherover, and Raible, but a real continental program in the same sense that A.U.Y. and U.Y.F. were continental programs seemed an unreachable goal. Many local chapters of the Channing Foundation thrived, however. In fact, from 1949 to 1951 the Tri-U group in Minneapolis was given the responsibility for co-ordinating the whole continental Channing Foundation Committee, but the minutes from that time report that the C.C.F.C. had "a pitiful existence".

June, 1950, saw the beginning of the Korean War, and another mobilization of college age people. The draft hurt the Murray Foundation program more than it did the Channing Foundation, because the Murray program was smaller and could ill afford to lose many of its leaders, this concern for college age people in the military is reflected in their minutes.

One reason these efforts never succeeded is that many of the college age leaders in both organizations were siphoned off into the regional and continental organizing of the high school aspect of the program. Another reason is that the regional organizations upon which the whole structure of the programs really relied were successful only in the mid-west and New England.

A third reason was, of course, money. The Universalists never could budget a serious sum towards college work, and the Unitarian effort was caught in the budget crunch as the Forties drew to a close.

Peter Raible, who did considerable work in the Midwest for the Channing Foundation, wrote a rather bitter memo in 1951 to Frank Ricker of the Pacific Central District blaming the failure of the Channing Foundation program on the lack of any significant funds to do the work. He pointed out that churches near campuses may be willing to help, but that ultimately they get no lasting benefit from such efforts. The students involved will eventually all move away.

One interesting development within the Channing and Murray local groups was the degree to which they included non-campus college age people. In 1948 thirty-four out of eighty-eight groups in the Channing Foundation Directory fell into that category. Many of the individuals in these groups were also not Unitarians. This appears to have been a bone of contention in some of those groups, as it is today in some L.R.Y. local groups. The 1948 Channing Foundation's College Guide notes:

"The relation of the local group to the church also depends a good deal on the proportion of Unitarians or non-Unitarians in the group... In the heavily divided or almost completely non-Unitarian group, the relationship of the group to the church has a tendency to be confused and difficult. The big point to remember is that non-Unitarian religious liberals have usually had an unpleasant experience in another church and do not want to be pushed towards church membership in any way...It is important, though, to make it clear that you are a Unitarian group. Many college groups de-emphasize this fact and make a great mistake. If we are really Unitarians, we should not hide that fact merely to appease a few potential members."

By 1951 when the merger process between the A.U.Y. and the U.Y.F. was in full swing, both the Channing and Murray foundations seemed on their last legs. The older members were increasingly looking upon the A.U.Y. and the U.Y.F. as high-school-aged organizations. The programs were merged into The Channing-Murray Foundation in 1953 and completely re-evaluated.

The Post-War U.Y.F.

Without a doubt the most important development within the Universalist Youth Fellowship after the end of World War II was the arrival on the scene of Alice Harrison. For over thirty years her career in the liberal church had centered around a ministry to young people. It was in the area of Junior High programming that Harrison's unique influence was felt, but one of the things that made her presence in the youth program so important was her ability to relate to young people of all ages.

Alice Harrison began her career in liberal religious education in the Universalist Church in Lynn, Massachusetts. She was involved in Y.P.C.U. events on the local and regional levels as an advisor from 1936. In 1945 she was hired by the Universalist Church of American as a staff person in the field of religious education. When Roger Bosworth resigned in 1946, Harrison became the U.C.A.'s Director of Youth Activities.

The Universalists had always been more inclusive of the junior high age people in their youth group than the Unitarians. Harrison's presence as Director of Youth Activities insured that the U.Y.F. program would continue to be a three-part one, relating to college age, high school, and junior high people. The lowering of the age of the Y.P.C.U. membership had come about more slowly than was the case with the Unitarians. When Fenn Leavitt took over as the last Y.P.C.U. president, he was in his early thirties. The change really happened from the bottom up. Because of the U.Y.F.'s smaller size, and because the U.Y.F. people were less politicized than the A.U.Y.ers, leaders tended to progress gradually through the ranks from the local level as they showed the interest and the talent.

As has been noted above, the U.Y.F. came out of the war years in reletively weak condition. By 1947-48, however, they had made a recovery at least financially and were operating with a budget of about five thousand dollars, not including Alice Harrison's salary. It proved necessary to discontinue U.Y.F. participation with the A.U.Y. in the publication of The Young Liberal, however. The magazine had increased in size and frequency from its original format, and overall costs for its publication had within one year become twice what was originally expected. At the 1947 U.Y.F. Annual Meeting, it was voted to discontinue the joint publication "purely for the purpose of strengthening our own organization." A major reason for the move was probably that the U.Y.F. could not hold up their end of the costs through subscriptions. Universalist subscriptions in the first part of 1947 were running twenty-to-one below Unitarian subscriptions. So for the kind of money they were required to put into the joint effort the Universalists were not getting a publication that benefited them. They returned to a publication of their own, entitled The Youth Leader.

The Youth Leader

Alice Harrison travelled a great deal as part of her job description, organizing and visiting groups on all three age levels of the U.Y.F. The

U.Y.F. leadership and board remained New England-centered, however. The
annual "New England Get-Together" Conference each February often drew
more people than the national convention. The "power blocs" within the
U.Y.F. were based in the state unions and the most populous and well-
organized state unions were the ones in New England, such as the Massachusetts-Rhode Island and Maine Unions.

The changing character of the U.Y.F. was reflected in a new set of
purposes passed at the 1948 Norway, Maine annual convention. The new
purposes replaced an old paragraph in the constitution entitled "Objects",
which read:

> The object of this fellowship shall be:
>
> The promotion of Christian culture, service, and
>
> leadership among the young people of the Universalist
>
> Church and the extension of the power and influence
>
> of liberalism in every way possible.

The six concise new purposes passed at that meeting make no mention
of the word "Christian" and contain no specific references to the Universalist Church. At the following year's annual meeting, a routine motion
of greeting to the Universalist Church of America was amended upon the
motion of Bill DeWolfe to eliminate the words: "its parent organization".

A Different Style

An institutional narrative of this period does not capture the
unmistakably different style and atmosphere of the youth movement in
the 1940's. The feel of the movement becomes more familiar to those
who have been involved with the L.R.Y. in more recent years.

The youth leaders begin to take time out from school to work full-
time for the youth organization. Field-tripping by the youth leadership

via hitch-hiking, rail, and for the first time, air, begins to happen.
David Parke spent two months at the beginning of 1948 in a long and thorough
field trip down the west coast of the United States and Canada. He arranged
to meet Dick Kuch and his 1948 Hudson ("a gorgeous hunk of automobile") in
Texas to drive back east.

Richard Woodman remembers well the travails of hitch-hiking to New
England U.Y.F. conferences. ("It took me twenty-five rides to get from
Boston to North Adams.") In the minutes of the 1949 convention of the
U.Y.F., we find the following resolution:

"Be it recommended that the U.Y.F. set up a commission which is to
form an independent organization to be called Hitchhikers International...
which will have as its purpose the promotion of safe and speedy hitch-
hiking by whatever means it sees fit."

A well-publicized event of the summer of 1948 was the A.U.Y. Caravan,
consisting of Leon Hopper, Carl Beck, and their magnificent Crosley automobile. They resolved to tour all the western A.U.Y. summer camps, and
made it, chugging 2600 miles from Tulsa, Oklahoma to Seattle, Washington,
back down to Asilomar in California, and finally back to Beck's home town
of Pittsburgh. They averaged eight miles an hour over the Rockies, and
the only major trouble they had was losing the fan belt through the
radiator on the way to Asilomar.

When Hopper lost a closely-contested election for A.U.Y. president
to Chuck Eddis in 1949, he decided to take time off from school anyway
and become an official A.U.Y. field director.

The 1948 American Unitarian Youth convention in Stillwater, Oklahoma
represented a major change in conference programming for the A.U.Y. It
was the first A.U.Y. convention to be held west of the Mississippi. Only

one hundred delegates were able to attend (compared to three hundred the year before at Star Island) because of the distances involved. It was also the first A.U.Y. convention to be held south of the Mason-Dixon line. That created a serious problem in the conference arrangements, for under state law at that time it was illegal for blacks and whites to share the same sleeping quarters. The college where the conference was being held was persuaded to bend its own segregation rules, but could not allow state laws to be violated in this regard. It was decided to hold the conference there regardless, and so Mildred Saunders, the A.U.Y. office secretary, who had been the first black person brought into the A.U.A. at any position other than maintenance staff, was forced to sleep down the road in a motel.

The Stillwater convention was also the first attempt at a week-long A.U.Y. convention. Being together for a week brought the summer camp experience and the A.U.Y. convention together. The conferences at that time had all the same kinds of rules problems that conferences today have. The rules around curfews and drinking were more explicit than they are today, and when violations occured there was usually more severe action taken. There were small furors around discussions of sexuality at Star Island in 1947, and about co-ed dorms at one of the Murray Grove conferences.

Part of the reason for adult concern about conferences, especially in the U.Y.F., was the presence of more junior high age people. The age range was such at these conventions that the sizable minority of people who were over twenty-one had to pledge abstinence from any possibly controversial behaviour. Ministers were more involved in these youth conferences than they are today. The guest speakers and workshop leaders

were often well-known ministers. One indication of a more relaxed attitude
towards youth conferences on the part of church leaders and their congregations appears in an A.U.Y. Young Liberal from 1950.[5] The issue has a
report on the first A.U.Y. Conference ever to sleep over the weekend
inside a church building. The site was Cincinnati, Ohio.

The Buildup to Merger

It is interesting to compare the size, the structure, and the style
of the two youth organizations in 1950, just as the merger process was
beginning. According to the Joint Relations Committee (which prepared
the merger plan) the two groups measured up as follows:

	A.U.Y.	U.Y.F.
Membership	2,432 approx.	4,000 approx.
No. of groups affiliated	221	246
Age Range	14-25 (av. 17)	12-25
Regional Distribution	New England 47% Mid Atlantic 13% Midwest 20% Other 20%	New England & N.Y. 55% Mid Atlantic 3% Midwest 22% Other 20%
Organization	Council of 20 w/ 4 elected officers 14 Regional Reps. 1 Past President 1 U.Y.F. Rep.	Board of 9 w/ 4 elected officers 4 Trustees representing task-oriented depts. 1 A.U.Y. Rep.

The fact that their joint publication only had a circulation of
1600 suggests that the membership figures above might have been a high
estimate, especially the U.Y.F. figure. It probably includes a sizeable
number of junior high people as well. Although the distribution of
members is almost the same in both groups, the A.U.Y's leadership and

strength was more evenly distributed across the continent.

Alice Harrison describes the American Unitarian Youth as a much more
highly politicized organization than the Universalist Youth Fellowship.[6]
Their size and their election procedures produced a very aggressive style
of leader and leadership, which made many of the U.Y.F. state conventions
nervous about the merger. Alice Harrison comments:

"The Unitarian youth, bless their hearts, could argue the Universalists
out of anything."[7]

Richard Woodman remembers the aura of solemnity and importance
around the Unitarian headquarters at 25 Beacon Street in the days of
Frederick Eliot. The first time he attended a meeting there representing
U.Y.F. on some joint committee he was very surprised to be given a voucher
to fill in for his personal expenses in making the trip down to Boston.
The A.U.Y. did have more money, reflecting their greater institutional
strength and that of the American Unitarian Association. The Universalist
congregations and youth groups were rural, rather than urban. U.Y.F.
leaders went to Tufts and St. Lawrence while the Unitarians were at Harvard
and Antioch.

On the other hand, the Universalists had a closer and more trusting
relationship to their adult denomination than did the Unitarians. The
U.C.A. leadership was younger than the A.U.A.'s, and their ties with the
youth were closer. The L.R.Y.'s first office after merger was located
at the Universalist headquarters at 16 Beacon Street rather than in the
larger Unitarian building at 25 Beacon Street.

The U.Y.F.'s withdrawal from the joint publication of The Young
Liberal had not indicated that the two youth groups had become alienated
from each other. On the contrary, interest in the possibility of merger

had never been greater. Merger was in the air in denominational terms as well. The 1947 American Unitarian Association convention had passed a resolution calling for an exploration of the possibility of merger with the Universalists. In 1949 a joint A.U.A.-U.C.A. Commission on Union was set up and at the time it appeared as if a merger within the following three years was imminent. The expectation proved to be premature, however. The final result of this commission was the establishment of the Council of Liberal Churches, which was to develop joint publications and publicity for the two denominations to supplement the co-operative religious education program that already existed.

It was in the summer of 1949 in this atmosphere of merger that the first steps towards the creation of Liberal Religious Youth were taken. At their summer annual meetings the American Unitarian Youth and the Universalist Youth Fellowship each passed resolutions inviting the other to hold their 1951 conferences and annual meetings together. Carl Seaburg was president of U.Y.F. during the year which preceded this resolution, while Charles Eddis was president of the A.U.Y.

A Joint Relations Committee consisting of six Unitarians, six Universalists, and the two staff people, Harrison and Henniges, was charged with planning that 1951 conference. At the 1950 annual meetings that committee was formally instructed to conduct a thorough exploration of the possibilities and process of a merger of the two groups, and to supervise the arrangements for the conference. During the two-year interval from these 1949 resolutions to the 1951 Joint Conference, U.Y.F. and A.U.Y. published a good deal of joint material on an experimental basis: a Youth Sunday guide, a Songbook, The Youth Leader, The Liberal's Challenge, as well as material explaining the plans and issues around merger.

Leon Hopper and Charles Collier served as Presidents of the A.U.Y. and the U.Y.F. respectively during the preparatory year of 1950-51.

The Creation of Liberal Religious Youth

The Joint Convention of 1951 was held at Camp Idlewild on an island in Lake Winnepesaukee, New Hampshire. The registration fee was eight dollars, and delegates from far away benefitted from a travel equalization fee.

The fact that the convention was on an island created some interesting situations. For one thing, the isolation of the camp promoted some justified concern about the degree to which the rules of conduct would be observed. Sure enough, a small party was discovered drinking on the backside of the island one night well after lights-out. The council supervising the conference had the unpleasant responsibility of asking the guilty parties to leave the island.

Both the American Unitarian Association and the Universalist Church of America were represented by their top leadership. Robert Cummins, Superintendent of the U.C.A., and Frederick May Eliot, the A.U.A. President, both addressed the convention in the middle of the week. Boat schedules made it necessary for Eliot to spend the night on the island. True to form, one of the skits presented during the A.U.Y.'s evening program featured a grand lampoon of President Eliot.

Both youth groups printed program material and information on each other and their respective denominations. The theme speaker for the week was Tracy Pullman, who was minister of the merged Universalist Unitarian Church of Detroit. Each organization met in a separate business session to discuss and vote on the report of the Joint Relations Committee.

The J.R.C. Report came in the form of a very well-balanced pro and

con statement. They did not recommend any rapid moves towards a merger.
Although they favored a fully organic union, they recommended it only
happen by a slow process taking at least three years. The report made
recommendations for local and regional interactions as well as executive-
level joint decision-making and co-operation. The J.R.C. expressed some
concern for continuity, and supported the continuation of an adult
professional staff and a youth-adult committee on the denominational level.
They argued that all appointments to these positions can be made by a
Personnel Committee composed of equal youth and adult representation.

The staff situation was of particular concern at this conference,
for the A.U.Y. Council asked for and received the resignation of Paul
Henniges as the A.U.Y. Director. The convention passed a controversial
resolution which read:

> Should at any time the staff situation become unfavor-
> able, the youth movement, after consultation with the
> Youth Activities Committee, shall have the power to
> discontinue the professional services of the staff member.

Eventually both groups endorsed in their separate sessions a two
year plan for merger, to culminate in 1953, with the Joint Relations
Committee and the two Executive Boards handling the transition. The
two Presidents elected to carry through the process were Rozelle Royall
for U.Y.F., and Leon Hopper, who was re-elected by the A.U.Y. The J.R.C.
was commissioned to prepare by-laws and program materials to facilitate
the merger, and the two groups voted to meet again in joint conventions
in 1952 and 1953. All the joint publications and consultations of the
two previous years were increased in this period.

In 1952 the A.U.Y. and A.U.A. announced the appointment of Sam Wright
as Executive Director of the A.U.Y. Wright held the job for three years,

throughout the merger period, becoming the first L.R.Y. Executive Director.
He authored the words to what became known as "The L.R.Y. Hymn". It was
(and occasionally still is) sung to the tune of "Finlandia" by Sibelius:

> We would be one, as now we join in singing
>
> Our hymn of youth, to pledge ourselves anew
>
> To that high cause of greater understanding
>
> Of who we are, and what in us is true.
>
> We would be one in living for each other
>
> To show mankind a new community.

> We would be one, in building for tomorrow
>
> A greater world than we have known today.
>
> We would be one, in searching for that meaning
>
> Which binds our hearts, and points us on our way
>
> As one we pledge ourselves to greater service,
>
> With love and justice strive to make men free.

In 1952 the A.U.Y.-U.Y.F. Joint Convention tentatively approved a
constitution for the merged organization, in spite of some concern on
the Universalist side that the process was happening too fast. The
leadership of both organizations worked furiously along on the merger
schedule.[9] The stage was set for the final vote.

The 1953 A.U.Y.-U.Y.F. Joint Convention was held at Hanover College,
Hanover, Indiana. The by-laws were reviewed and revised and further discussions were held. The final formal merger votes were held in separate
business sessions. Alice Harrison recalls that the whole discussion took
seven hours, "without eating, without sleeping, without hardly getting up
to go to the john", before they arrived at that final vote at Hanover.

The Universalist side still expressed a little reluctance, registering a 47 "yes" - 4 "no" votes. Of the four negative votes, some had been cast per the instructions of their local group or church. Both sides, however, voted overwhelmingly in favor of merger. In joint session, they made the motion formally unanimous.

There was a little bit of difficulty with the name for the new organization, however. Beyond the concerns of some in each group about losing their denominational identities, the Canadians were reluctant to endorse the title "Liberal Religious" because of the possible confusion with the Canadian Liberal Party. The name"Liberal Religious Youth" was by far the most popular choice, however, and Liberal Religious Youth it became.

Over the two years since the joint conference of 1951, the A.U.Y. and U.Y.F. governing bodies had been meeting together and making decisions in joint session as much as possible. Rozelle Royall had served as U.Y.F. president throughout the merger process, with Eileen Layton taking over from Leon Hopper as A.U.Y. president in 1952-53.

L.R.Y.'s first continental convention and its incorporation as a separate successor organization did not occur until 1954. The A.U.Y. and U.Y.F. boards continued to exist and to function in a parallel fashion until then, but for all intents and purposes the new merged Executive Board structure began functioning after the 1953 conference.

The new board structure incorporated the basic A.U.Y. structure with features of the U.Y.F. There were four officers elected by the convention, but they were elected to staggered two-year terms. Filling out the governing board were seventeen regional representatives sent by their respective regions. Clara Mayo was elected the first president of L.R.Y. She had been the last A.U.Y. president in 1953-54.

With all these merger plans in process, the two college age programs associated with the A.U.Y. and the U.Y.F. also merged, becoming the Channing-Murray Foundation.

There was one further problem in deciding what the age limits of the new L.R.Y. would be. Twenty-five was certainly to be the top age limit, but what about the junior high people? In a compromise move, it was decided that voting members of L.R.Y. were to be fourteen to twenty-five years old, although local groups could include members as young as twelve.

After the Hanover convention ended, a group of these new L.R.Y.'ers travelled forty strong to Andover, Massachusetts, where the representatives of the Unitarian and Universalist churches were meeting in joint session trying to bring into being the Council of Liberal Churches. The LRYers made a presentation concerning their merger process and contributed greatly to the spirit and the work of that gathering.

With the merger, L.R.Y. adopted a more cordial relationship with the professional staff and with the two denominations. Staff was hired by a Joint Personnel Committee and paid from A.U.A. and U.C.A. money. Sam Wright became the Executive Director of L.R.Y., with Alice Harrison becoming Associate Director for High School Programs, and Eileen Layton, Associate Director for College Activities (i.e. the Channing Murray Foundation.)[10]

The creation of L.R.Y. was not only a significant event in the history of the liberal youth movement. It is important in the history of Unitarian and Universalism as a whole, for it showed the Unitarian and Universalist churches that had been dancing about the maypole of merger for years that a merger could be successfully accomplished, and perhaps more important, that it was inevitable.

For the youth, it was the beginning of new era. As Leon Hopper
observed:

"With the completion of a successful merger, and augmented by an
independent staff (responsible to the L.R.Y. Council) the theme of
"Youth Autonomy" and independence became even stronger." [11]

CARL SEABURG REMEMBERS NORWAY, MAINE - 1950's.

In the years around 1950, the First Universalist Church in Norway, Maine had a vigorous youth program going. Norway was a town of 5,000 people then, some 45 miles in from Portland on the coast and not too near any large city. A few shoe factories were its main industry and it proudly called itself the Snowshoe Capital of the World. A large lake on the edge of the town attracted many summer people. One of the local wits achieved some notoriety for his retort to one of the summer people who asked him what the townspeople did after the visitors left. "We fumigate," was his terse reply.

The Universalist and Congregational churches were the principal Protestant churches in the community, with small Baptist, Methodist, and Episcopal chapels serving their communicants. The single Roman Catholic church served several surrounding towns. A considerable settlement of Finns had a generation or so earlier moved into the area and added a special flavor to the region.

When the present writer came to this town at the end of the second World War, he found an active Junior High youth program with some 15 youngsters under the capable lay leadership of Mrs. Ruth Russell. Shortly after his arrival a high school youth program was started and the group decided to call itself the Norway Universalist Youth, or NUY for short. An active church school, a cub scout program, an off-again, on-again Boy Scout troop, and occasionally a Junior Choir of youngsters to supplement the adult Senior Choir completed the youth program of the church during most of the years under review.

From 30 to 50 youngsters took part in the two youth groups, moving

almost automatically from one to the other. Each group developed tradi-
tions which continued year after year and became events looked forward
to by the members. Both groups were active participants in the statewide
youth programs of the denomination, with carloads attending all the
various youth rallies held in the state. One memorable occasion was the
250 mile trek from Norway to Caribou in the northernmost part of the
state for a three-day youth gathering that was happily remembered for
many seasons. Three or four of these state rallies would be attended
each year. Since Ferry Beach was in Maine, a goodly number of the
youth group members attended summer youth programs there and looked
forward to the annual Ferry Beach reunion in the spring.

New England youth meetings were also attended by a smaller number
and in August 1949, the Norway youth groups hosted the 60th national
convention of the Universalist Youth Fellowship. This involved much
planning on the part of the hosts and featured the usual business
sessions, workshops, a carnival, a beaching outing at the lake, a grand
ball, and a street dance when the town blocked off the main street and
joined in the festivities with their weekend visitors. One hundred
fifteen young people were registered, and a great many others were around
for the affair.

The Junior High Fellowship ordinarily met on Sundays at 5 p.m. and
once a month had a supper which they prepared themselves, with a little
guidance from their advisors who had to eat the repast too. A lot of
physical activity marked their programs. A look at the old folders
shows in any one year that the group would go rollerskating at the local
rink, swimming at the Hebron Academy pool, bowling, folk dancing, dancing
at a record party, climbing some of the local "mountains," hiking on

Sunday afternoons to interesting local spots, and the like.

They visited other nearby local Universalist youth groups and invited them back to their meetings. Speakers came in on topics which might have some appeal at their level of interests. There might be a debate on the value of comic books (a hot issue then!), the Mormon elders might be invited over, a filmstrip on the U.N. would be shown, and so on. Sometimes they would have a "home talent" night or visit one of the local industries. Always a short worship service led by one of the members preceed the evening activities.

The NUY meeting Sundays at 7 p.m. repeated the pattern of many of these programs with some additional items. One of their eagerly antici- pated events was the annual winter trip when the whole group (after raising money to pay for it) went off on a long weekend that included skiing, toboganning, snowshoeing, building snow forts and having snowball fights outside and much card playing, bull sessions, horsing around, and general good fun inside. One year they camped out in a parishioner's cabin to which the only access was across a frozen lake. Supplies had to be towed in on a toboggan, and drinking water had to be chopped out of the lake. Several years in a row they went up to Gilead to Si and Mary Cole's place. Mary's good cooking and Si's fiddle livened up the time spent there. Coming home the first time we went there we were treated to a magnificent display of the aurora borealis, the first time many of us had seen this spectacular sky event.

Another annual event was their Minstrel Show. Given in traditional blackface the first year, the minister had a problem with this which was talked over candidly within the group. Their solution for succeeding shows was to present the Minstrel Show in other guises. Holding to the basic pattern of a minstrel show - with an interlocuter, end men (ah, the sexist days of old!), a chorus, specialties, and a barrelful of corny jokes - they presented in succession a circus minstrel, a Gay Nineties minstrel, a Western minstrel, a Braodway minstrel, and so on.

Started by Mrs. Ernestine Brown, advisor of the NUY, these were ably assisted by Bess Klain and Vern Whitman as the sparkling pianists. The younger youth group joined the NUY for this annual shindig and looked forward to the time when they could take some of the leading parts. Tickets were only 50¢ (which went a lot further then) and audiences of 200 or more would be attracted. Often there would be a quarter of that number up on stage singing their lungs out.

Deep intellectual meetings were in short supply, unfortunately, much to the regret of the minister, though some attempts were made in this direction. Fun and fellowship were the strong points, and the social message had to wiggle in the back door. For instance, one night the NUY had a "Chinese Night" with the JrHi Fellowship as their guests. Everyone attending had to take off their shoes at the door. The committee sported kimonos. The worship service included an old Chinese folksong, the reading of Taoist, Confucianist, and Buddhist scriptures, and concluded with ahearty rendering of "In Christ There Is No East or West." The meal was eaten sitting cross-legged on the floor. Subsequently a Finnish evening and a Pennsylvania Dutch evening were planned. These events took a lot of preparation but were greatly enjoyed.

One useful by-product of this active participation of the youth in the life of the church was that many of the young men of the high school group, starting with Stanton Anderson, served as janitor to the church and provided splendid custodial care.

Looking back after 25 years, it would seem that an active happy social life was provided that reached out and embraced many who had not previously been associated with that Universalist church. A number of them who stayed on in the community are still active in its concerns today.

Chapter 7: L.R.Y. COMES OF AGE

There was now one youth organization bearing the responsibility for high school and college programming for two denominations. The American Unitarian Association and the Universalist Church of America each contributed to L.R.Y.'s budget, supporting it together at slightly less than the current level. Having two separate denominational bureaucracies with which to relate might have made communication between youth and adults more complicated than it usually is. A Joint Youth Advisory Committee composed of Unitarian and Universalist leaders and L.R.Y.ers was set up to faciliate communication and co-operation in funding and programming.

The first Continental Convention of Liberal Religious Youth was held in 1954 at Chesire Academy, Chesire, Connecticut. It was followed by the International Religious Fellowship's annual conference, which was being held in America for the first time since 1936.

I.R.F. and the Founding of Albert Schweitzer College

After Chuck Eddis's involvement with the A.U.Y. decreased, contact with the I.R.F. was maintained mainly through the efforts of Eileen Layton. Layton was the A.U.Y.'s official delegate to the 1951 I.R.F. conference in Switzerland. This began an association with I.R.F. which lasted until Eileen left L.R.Y.'s employ in 1957. When she went to Europe again in 1952 under A.U.Y.'s sponsorship she was elected second vice-president of I.R.F.[1] Her efforts brought the 1954 conference to America, and she organized a three month program of touring and study for the eleven Europeans who came over for that conference at Chesire.

There were two major issues that marked this period in I.R.F.'s history. The first was one that went right to the heart of I.R.F.'s understanding of itself and its purposes.

After the Second World War ended, the free religious congregations of Germany reorganized themselves and re-established their international contacts. The first post-war I.R.F. gathering in England had extended a special resolution of support and goodwill to German youth but no meaningful contact was made until 1950. As the new youth groups in these churches developed, they identified with the broad liberal religious orientation of the free religious congregations with which they were affiliated.

Ruth Neuendorffer of America made the first official contact with the German groups, and I.R.F. president Ronald McGraw of England was instrumental in arranging a tour of England for the Offenbach Free Religous Youth in 1951. Later in the summer of 1951 the Germans applied for membership in the I.R.F. as a united group calling themselves "Freireligiouse Jugenbund Deutschlands" (The Free Religious Youth Group of Germany – F.J.D.).

The strongest member groups of the I.R.F. at that time were the Swiss "Zwinglibund" and the Dutch group. Both groups were affiliated with the Free Christian or Free Protestant churches in their countries which maintained their identity as Christians. They were unwilling to consider the admission to I.R.F. of non-Christian groups. When the issue came to the floor of the business meeting in 1951 it was tabled with no conclusive decision reached.

Eileen Layton brought a report of the meeting back to the 1951-52 A.U.Y. Council meetings over Christmas, 1951. The Council was very much in favour of expanding I.R.F. from an exclusively Christian group to include all other "liberal religious groups", and had indicated this in resolutions

at previous meetings and at the conventions of 1950,1951, and again in 1952.
Finally in 1953, the F.J.D. was voted in as a member group of I.R.F. after
a year of written communication about the matter. It was an important
move in opening up the I.R.F. to include the broader definition of
"liberal religion" that was more common in America.

Another project that I.R.F.'ers became deeply involved in at this
time was the founding of Albert Schweitzer College in Switzerland. In
1949, Professor Hans Casparis of Chur, Switzerland, who was himself an
old I.R.F.'er, began a summer study camp which he called Modern International College (M.I.C.). He wanted to build M.I.C. into a fully-accredited
year-round college providing a broader undergraduate liberal education
than was then available in larger established schools. I.R.F. supported
the idea morally and financially. The I.R.F. member groups had a fund-
raising quota to reach for the support of the college.

By 1952 there was an attempt to merge the Secretariat of the I.R.F.
with Modern International College and make it a permanent Secretariat in
Switzerland. This was an idea the Americans had long favored. However,
it did not work out, for M.I.C. finally acquired its own building. On
May 5, 1953, the college purchased a thirty room hotel in Churwalden,
Switzerland for about ten thousand dollars. Having established a home
and a program, Prof. Casparis approached Dr. Albert Schweitzer for
permission to name the college after him. Schweitzer was delighted to
give his blessing, and so in the fall of 1953, Albert Schweitzer College
opened its doors with twenty-five people from five countries enrolled
in its program.

The college program concentrated on small classes, with informal
but intensive study groups under the tutelage of a professor-advisor.

The undergraduate program was a two-year interdisciplinary study of Western civilization in all its facets. Many I.R.F. and L.R.Y. people were involved in Albert Schweitzer College over the course of its existence. At its first summer study session in 1953, some twenty-three Americans were present, including Eileen Layton and Sam Wright.

Staff Relations

At the first L.R.Y. Continental Convention at Chesire, Connecticut, the youth leadership and the conference delegates called the professional staff on the carpet during the annual meeting. In effect they were asking them to justify their jobs and the manner in which they had been performing them.[2]

It had been a hot day and a long meeting, and everyone was a little cranky. Sam Wright and Eileen Layton got up and gave a verbal account of their work above and beyond the written report they had handed in. Then it was Alice Harrison's turn. As she remembered it, she stood up in front of the convention and said quietly:

"You have my report. I don't know what else to say, except that never before in my professional career has anyone ever asked me to defend the job I've given my life to. So I have nothing to say."[3]

No one else had anything more to say either. The matter was dropped and the meeting moved on to other things, but with a feeling that the air had been cleared.

Apparently it hadn't been completely cleared, for in the fall of 1954, Sam Wright accepted a call back to the parish ministry and resigned his position as L.R.Y. Executive Director. A personnel committee was set up with representation from both denominations. The leadership of L.R.Y. at this point still tended to be college students. A few had undergone

two years of military service which had interrupted their L.R.Y. careers.
Their top age might be twenty-two years old.

The pattern that had been followed in hiring adult staff and advisors
for the A.U.Y. in the past had been one of seeking out parish ministers
who seemed appropriately qualified and attempting to lure them to this
nice Boston-based job with lots of travel opportunities. The personnel
committee that met in late 1954 decided that what they really wanted was
a person with a lot of experience in the development of youth programs,
even if that person had to be found outside the denomination. The person
they eventually did choose, Bill Gold, did come from outside the Unitarian
Universalist fold. His experience and objective insight into L.R.Y.'s
situation was, in many ways, just what they needed. However, it would
not be long before this hopeful situation would begin to go sour.

Gold began work in early 1955, joining Alice Harrison and Eileen
Layton on the professional staff. The Continental Convention was held
that year in Olivet, Michigan. Robert Johnson was elected L.R.Y. President
for the year to come.

L.R.Y. Inc.

Since the merger had been completed L.R.Y. had been having difficulty
with its corporate status. Originally, the question of where to incorporate
had been an issue, because Massachusetts law requires corporations registered
there to hold their annual meetings in Massachusetts. The necessity of
holding the annual meeting along with the Continental Convention, wherever
that might turn out to be, made the L.R.Y. incorporators decide in 1953
to register the corporation in the state of Delaware, where no such
requirement existed. However, the Massachusetts state legislature refused to allow the invested capital of the A.U.Y. and the U.Y.F. to be

transferred to a Delaware corporation.

The L.R.Y. Council therefore decided to petition the Massachusetts legislature to make an exception to its corporate laws due to the circumstances of L.R.Y.'s operations. The petition was accepted, and in 1956, L.R.Y. was finally incorporated in Massachusetts under a special act of the Massachusetts legislature.

Over the first few annual meetings the new L.R.Y. Council fell into a pattern of doing business which would remain fairly stable over the following twelve years. The L.R.Y. by-laws specified the basic regional divisions from which the council representatives would be drawn. These regional groupings divided and subdivided into separate federations as L.R.Y. grew, but the voting distribution set up by the early Council remained stable.

The Council structured its meetings so that topic-oriented Commissions did most of the ground work in their respective areas during the week of Council meetings. At the end of the week each commission would come back with a series of specific recommendations for the whole Council to consider and vote on. This structure was maintained from 1954 through the L.R.Y. Board meetings of 1968.

The Channing - Murray Program

After the initial flurry of activity in programming for college age people during the late 1940's, the whole area was again neglected for a couple of years. In 1947-48 the Channing Foundation of the A.U.Y. had some eighty-eight groups registered with them. By 1953 when L.R.Y. came into being, there were only fifteen left. The Universalists had even fewer, and they only kept in touch with them by mail.

The most consistent programming for college students continued to come out of the churches themselves on a regional and local basis. The Western Unitarian Conference set up its own College Centers Committee in 1951, and the Channing Foundation co-operated with existing college programs in the Metropolitan Area Council (New York), in Maine, and in the Boston area.

When L.R.Y. was created, Eileen Layton was given specific responsibility for the new Channing-Murray program. The Liberal's Challenge continued as a regular college age periodical under her supervision. By 1955, after two years of organizing, the number of existing Channing-Murray groups was back up to around eighty-nine. This represented the peak of the program, for when Eileen Layton left the L.R.Y. staff in 1957 the program could not be maintained and it slipped back again.

By far the most successful campus-based program within Channing - Murray was in Urbana, Illinois. Arnold Westwood, himself a former A.U.Y. President, and minister in the Urbana Church, began the program along with Earl McKinney. They raised money from area churches and received grants from the A.U.A. During the fifties their budget averaged around $1,250. a year, and supported a staff of three, one of them working full-time.

The program has continued up until the present day. It has involved topic-oriented seminars among the members, well-known guest speakers on the campus and at the church, social events, and a regular coffee house called The Red Herring.

Local programs like these flourished on their own with the help of interested ministers and a good core of student leaders, but in the early 1950's only New England, Ohio, and Illinois developed regional activity of any kind.

As early as the late 1940's there had been talk of separating the

college age programming from the basic high school orientation of L.R.Y.
In 1953, in her Channing - Murray report, Eileen Layton commented:

"A.U.Y. is sadly deficient in its college approach; is A.U.Y. really
two organizations, High School and College, in one, and if it is, shouldn't
we recognize it as such?" Although the American Unitarian Association
began to take a more direct hand in promoting college work in the late
1950's this whole area continued to be a point of tension with L.R.Y.

This tension was reflected in a motion passed at the 1957 L.R.Y.
Continental Convention. It created two councils within L.R.Y., one high
school and one college-age, with biennial continental conventions and
separate leadership training conferences in the interim. This plan
eventually proved ineffective and was superceded by other ideas. However,
it did tend to create separate programming for the two groups within the
structure of the continental convention.

Bill Gold Resigns

On May 27, 1956, Bill Gold submitted his resignation as Executive
Director of L.R.Y. after only fifteen months in that position. He resigned
to accept a call into the parish ministry. The decision was a blow to
the L.R.Y. leadership. They placed blame upon themselves for the tensions
and the shortcomings in Gold's relationship with them and with L.R.Y. as
an organization, as is reflected in the resolution they passed after
formally receiving Gold's resignation letter in the summer of 1956:

> Whereas, there has been insufficient communication
> among the staff members, and
> Whereas the personal relations among leaders of L.R.Y.
> have been overstressed, and
> Whereas these shortcomings may have hindered the realization

of L.R.Y.'s stated programs,

Be is resolved, that L.R.Y. recognize these errors

and strive to overcome them.[4]

Certainly, the youth leadership had not been able to listen to Bill Gold's concerns, and had not been able to follow the directions in which he wanted to move. However, there were factors beyond that involved in his decision to resign.

For one thing, Gold came from outside the denomination into a working situation with an inherited staff (Harrison and Layton) who had a closer relationship with, and understanding of L.R.Y. The way the concept of "youth autonomy" had functioned in L.R.Y. had been as more of an ideological backdrop than a well-defined blueprint for responsibility and decision making. Gold understood youth autonomy in L.R.Y. intellectually, but could never strike the right balance of power in his relationship to the Executive Committee and the Council. Neither side could find ways to communicate their position adequately to the other.

As for his relationship with the two denominations, Gold faced the same frustrations as every succeeding Executive Director was to face. L.R.Y.'s size and needs were clearly growing, and the financial support offered by the U.C.A. and the A.U.A. was not enough to keep up with it. Many of Gold's ideas and goals were out of reach due to lack of funds. At the time of his resignation, the U.C.A. was forced to cut back their support even further, so that the 1956 Council could see that Alice Harrison's resignation from job was imminent. She left the following year to work within the new Junior High program of the Council of Liberal Churches.

Gold left L.R.Y. to accept a call to the pulpit of the church in Schenectady, New York. His letter of resignation, final report, and some

"brief observations" that he wrote as the job ended indicate that many
of the problematic themes that would plague L.R.Y. up until today existed
full-blown in the mid-fifties. A particular concern of his was the
tension between L.R.Y.'s role as a "service organization" for the youth
of the Unitarian and Universalist denominations, and its significance
as an experience-centered extended family:

> It has been my conviction that L.R.Y.'s program must go
> beyond the experience-centered type of program it has
> had in the past, important as this emphasis is. I have
> therefore sought to make my work with L.R.Y. as much as
> possible a work of rendering services to local churches...
> feeling that otherwise L.R.Y. would become an organization
> offering a limited experience to a limited number of
> youth leaders.

There are some in our churches who perceive the changes L.R.Y. underwent in the late sixties as being due to a "takeover" of L.R.Y.'s structure
by young people more alienated from and distrustful of the social milieu
they grew up in than L.R.Y.ers had been in the past. I am struck by how
much some of Gold's observations of 1956 zero in on problems that have
continued to exist in L.R.Y.:

> Many of the most devoted young people lack the kind of
> experience which would make their devotion to L.R.Y.
> truly invaluable. They have never had the experience
> of being in a strong local group or of participating
> in a complete and well-organized youth program. To them
> the liberal religious youth group is a source of security
> in their eccentricity. This is a valuable contribution

the group should make to youth who might otherwise
be lonely in their individuality, but if it is the
dominant force in the life of the group or the
individual, it results in a distorted concept of
L.R.Y.'s program and purposes. Young people with
such a background are more likely to be more
concerned about maintaining the organization
and manipulating the structure than about developing
its program and advancing its fundamental purposes.
This is a logical concern since they lack the
knowledge and experience to develop programs and
they are primarily concerned with preserving the
structure that has made them feel significant.
However, if L.R.Y. is to carry the burden of liberal
religious education for the entire youth of two
great denominations, it must do more than preserve
its unique organization.[6]

Gold left the L.R.Y. Council with a number of recommendations.
They included more leadership training for L.R.Y. Leaders on the local
and regional levels; a separation of the college and high school programs;
encouraging more sympathetic interest in and support for L.R.Y.'s programming
on the part of adults; and a budget of at least thirty-five to forty
thousand dollars with three professional staff and two secretaries.

With Alice Harrison's resignation also upon them, and finances so

bad, the Council decided to request Eileen Layton's resignation from the
staff also in order to begin again with a clean slate.

The year 1956-57 saw much introspection and review on the part of
L.R.Y.'s leadership. They established a Committee on Planning and Review,
with youth and adult membership in addition to the personnel committee
which was searching for a new Executive Director. The Joint Youth
Activities Committee took a strong hand in filling the gap that year,
as did a special Council of Liberal Churches - L.R.Y. Committee which
particularly investigated the relation between the high school and
college programs of L.R.Y.

The 1957 L.R.Y. Continental Convention went by with no announcement
of the new Executive Director. Richard Teare was elected as L.R.Y.
President that year. That fall the appointment of Leon Hopper as L.R.Y.
Executive Director was finally confirmed.

New Directions

Leon Hopper began work officially in December, 1957, although as a
member of the Liberal Religious Youth Advisory Committee he had been on
hand for the Midwinter Council Meetings and the 1957 Jones Gulch Annual
Conference. He was twenty-nine years old at the time, and only six years
away from his own L.R.Y. leadership experiences.

Hopper's first report to the L.R.Y. Council at their winter meetings
was a strong statement that set the tone for his six years with L.R.Y.
He was responsible for services to high school and college age youth of
two denominations in six hundred churches, with a full-time staff of one
Director and one secretary, and a $27,000 budget. Hopper went on to indict
L.R.Y.'s present predicament:

...the fact is that L.R.Y. has not produced - it has not captured

the interest and support of our churches which it should
have, it has not made a mark on the high school youth, it
has barely touched the college student. You have not been
able to attract the professional leadership you need - you
have not been able to provide the resources demanded, or
render the services requested...To be very frank, L.R.Y.
is entering a period of trial...It is my strong feeling
that L.R.Y. is in a rut - that the ways in which it has done
things in the past will not be adequate to meet the demands
of our new responsibilities. L.R.Y. is going to have to be
willing to use new approaches - to revolutionize itself.

He proposed at that Council Meeting a four-point policy on program
production which established the pattern L.R.Y. followed in its printed
programs through the Sixties. Hopper's recommendation was that L.R.Y.
commit itself to producing a variety of program resource materials for
use by local groups, with the major responsibility for development of
these materials to rest with the Executive Director. He asked that the
Council make budgeting provisions for the editorial development as well
as production of these materials, looking towards an end goal that the
sale of materials would cover the cost of production.

Hopper was dissatisfied with the kind of communication problems
existing between the Continental Convention and the Council. He made
it clear to the Council what his particular skills were, what goals he
had, and he asked for a free hand and support in accomplishing them.
His relationships with the five L.R.Y. Executive Committees and Councils
he worked with seem to have been mutually satisfying. The kind of
continuity and vision Leon Hopper provided was something that L.R.Y. badly

needed at that time, and it showed results in the growth spurt L.R.Y. went through during his tenure. That growth period was partly a reflection of the growth in the adult denomination, but it also represented better organization and communication between Boston and the local and regional groups.

New L.R.Y. groups and federations came into existence, and more of them began to affiliate and pay dues. In the whole six-year period the number of active federations in L.R.Y. grew from twenty-one to thirty-three. Some of this growth was a result of the expansion and splitting apart of old federations. A result of these developments was the establishment of more regional committees to co-ordinate activities in a geographic area where there were a number of federations. The New England Regional Committee (N.E.R.C.) had existed in A.U.Y. since 1946, and new regionals modelled after N.E.R.C. began springing up. MICON (the Midwest's regional committee) was established in October, 1958, at a large meeting in Chicago, and was soon followed by M.A.R.C. (the Middle Atlantic Regional Committee) and the South East L.R.Y.

I.R.F. Returns to America

The summer of 1958 was an important year for L.R.Y.'s international involvement. Only eleven Europeans had come to America for the first L.R.Y. - I.R.F. joint conference in 1954. However, through the efforts of Eileen Layton a full contingent of thirty L.R.Y.ers went to Europe the following summer to participate in the 1955 I.R.F. Conference in Barnston, England. Layton functioned that year as I.R.F.'s "Advisor"and operated the I.R.F. Secretariat out of Boston.

Gradually the American goal of a more democratic I.R.F. structure was being achieved. During Layton's I.R.F. involvement, a nominating

141

committee was elected for the first time, and the Commissions at conferences were expanded so that all delegates could participate. The I.R.F.
Executive Committee began to meet at mid-year in addition to their annual
meeting in conjunction with the conference.

There was a big buildup and careful planning within L.R.Y. for the
1958 American I.R.F. Conference. It was to be held in Madison, Wisconsin,
in conjunction with the sixteenth Congress of the International Association
for Religious Freedom. Spencer Lavan was the co-ordinator of the arrangements. Twenty-seven Europeans made the journey to America, and L.R.Y.
organized a thirty day tour of the United States and Canada in private
automobiles for them.

The tour ended at the I.A.R.F. Congress. The I.R.F. Conference,
with the theme "Social Welfare: Who Cares?", followed it. In all, seventy-
six delegates from seven countries were in attendence. After the conference,
many of the participants migrated south to Guilford College in Guilford,
North Carolina, for the 1958 L.R.Y. Convention. There Spencer Lavan was
elected president of L.R.Y.

The admission of the German group, Freireligiose Jugenbund Deutschlands
and the general liberalizing tendency within I.R.F. continued to produce
changes within its membership. The Dutch group (V.C.J.C.) was becoming
less and less committed to I.R.F. and by the beginning of the Sixties
was only paying minimal membership dues. A group of "Dutch Friends of
I.R.F." was taking a more active role at conferences. The humanist
element in the F.J.D. finally split off from the rest of the organization
and began to associate with the youth organization of the International
Humanist and Ethical Union. These were mostly groups in northern Germany.
The groups in the area of Frankfurt, Mainz, and Offenbach continued their

I.R.F. affiliation, and in the late Fifties, a new group in the south
of Germany, "Freichristliche Jugenbund" (F.C.J.) came into I.R.F.

Albert Schweitzer College continued its program, but without the
same kind of close ties with I.R.F. that had existed at its inception.

The Development Fund and College Centers

The American Unitarian Association had a College Centers Committee
dating from the 1940's. It co-operated with the programs A.U.Y. and L.R.Y.
had going, but met with the same limited success. Sociological analyses
of the membership of the A.U.A. would invariably announce that the colleges
were a gold mine of potential members; that the college years were a time
for seeking one's religious identity, and questioning the religious environment that one had been raised in; and that the A.U.A. was really
missing the boat in its approach to college programming.

In 1956 an opportunity arose to see if these theories were true.
The General Alliance of Unitarian Women had raised a special Diamond
Jubilee Fund of $18,000.00 which they wished to donate to the American
Unitarian Association. At the suggestion of Frederick Eliot, it was
earmarked for college work. The College Centers Committee was revived
and reconstituted as a foundation which made grants to local college
centers programs. They also administered the Billings Fund, which was
given to sponsor lectures on college campuses. Under C.C.C. the lectures
were particularly directed at colleges with a strong Unitarian presence.

The College Centers Committee operated independently of the Channing
Murray Foundation, for that was Unitarian and Universalist. However,
there was a further influx of funds into college programming which would
bring the two programs closer together. Frederick Eliot died suddenly
on February 17, 1958, with three years left in his unexpired term. Dana

McLean Greeley was elected President of the A.U.A. on May 1, 1958.
Greeley inaguurated a giant financial campaign entitled The Development
Fund. It was to be money raised mostly for program purposes, rather
than as endowment capital. The Development Fund pledged $250,000.00
towards college work, to be given over a period of years.

Nothing like this sum of money was ever spent, but the first fruit
of the proposal was that Leon Hopper was able to get the extra staff
member he had been wanting. In 1959 Orloff Miller was hired as Associate
Director of L.R.Y. with a major responsibility in college work. Miller
was to work closely with the College Centers Committee and serve as
their Secretary. Miller became the only staff person in touch with all
three prongs of Unitarian college programming (College Centers, Channing-
Murray, and the local and regional College Centers.)

A major problem with the College Centers approach had to do with
evaluation. Grants were given left and right, and local programs began
and flourished, but it was very difficult to determine the degree to
which these programs influenced the students view of liberal religion.
The primary motive behind these programs as far as the A.U.A. was
concerned was extension, based on the thesis that colleges were a ripe
orchard of new members. The period from 1958-1969 represents the most
successful approach to college programming in the history of the youth
movement, but no one is really sure what lasting effect it had on the
individuals involved or on the U-U movement as a whole.

L.R.Y. and the Unitarian-Universalist Merger

For the first six years of L.R.Y.'s existence it had been like the
child of divorced parents. Both parents supported Junior and both had
ideas about how Junior should spend the money. It must have been an awkward
situation in some ways.

By 1959 merger fervor in the two denominations was higher than it had ever been. The machinery had finally been set in motion to bring the whole issue to some resolution. The future of L.R.Y. in a new merged denomination was a matter of some anxiety to L.R.Y. leaders. During this period, L.R.Y. used well its Committee on Planning and Review. This committee was like a Commission of Appraisal within L.R.Y., and solicited opinions concerning the organization's work from an adult advisory group of old A.U.Y. - U.Y.F. -L.R.Y. members. The participants regularly received a set of questions regarding L.R.Y., and everyone's written reflections on the questions would be compiled, summarized, and distributed.

During 1958-59 this committee went through a process of evaluating the successes and failures of the L.R.Y. merger, while at the same time looking ahead to the inevitable merger of the two adult denominations and what consequences that might have for L.R.Y.

Leon Hopper saw the occasion as a time of testing for L.R.Y. He saw many issues that could be dealt with as all the old structures were re-examined in the light of merger. A major one was the old tension of being fundamentally a high school organization run by college students. Another was the excessive amount of staff time lost in simple maintenance of the institution of L.R.Y. It sapped energy from programming work. These issues were raised and discussed at the 1959 L.R.Y. Continental Convention at Grinnell College, Grinnell, Iowa.

Hopper had clear ideas about the kind of relationship with the denomination which would best deal with these problems and put L.R.Y. into a much better position in terms of denominational funding and interest. He recommended first a much closer relationship with the denomination on all levels; in particular the incorporation of the L.R.Y.

professional staff into the Department of Education of the new denomination
where there was more status, job security, and stability. Secondly he
suggested that the high school and college age programs be separated.
Thirdly, he recommended that the old Council structure be overhauled,
since it duplicated and paralleled tasks that could be done by the new
regional committee organizations.

The American Unitarian Association and the Universalist Church of
America voted to merge in 1961 into the Unitarian Universalist Association.
Hopper's recommendations for structuring the new U.U.A. - L.R.Y. relationships were substantially accepted by all concerned. The L.R.Y. Executive
Director became part of the staff of the new Division of Education, paid
out of their budget. A new Liberal Religious Youth Advisory Committee
was established.

The L.R.Y. council was abolished and the continental board of trustees
which exists now was created in its place. The council had been composed
of twenty representatives from "regional groupings" which no longer
reflected L.R.Y.'s federation structure. The new board was to be composed
of the presidents or representatives of each dues-paying federation.
The executive committee was realigned also to include three directors
in addition to the usual four officers. This new board controlled the
funds L.R.Y. received from dues and investment income while the rest of
L.R.Y.'s money all went through the Division of Education budget and was
used for salaries, office expenses, and staff travel. The total budget
L.R.Y. used amounted to between twenty-three and twenty-five thousand
dollars.

The L.R.Y. annual convention was also abolished and renamed the
"Continental Conference", reflecting a new emphasis on program rather

than business-oriented conferences. The final major change that occured
with the denominational merger was that L.R.Y. voted to become an organization for high school students. The by-laws of L.R.Y. were rewritten
to accomodate the new board structure, and included within those by-laws
were age limits of fourteen to nineteen years. A person could be elected
to the executive committee up to his or her sophmore year in college,
but not beyond.[9]

The Creation of S.R.L.

The final separation of the high school program from the college
program within L.R.Y. arose out of nearly fifteen years of frustration
on the part of college age people. L.R.Y. had been substantially a high
school organization from its inception in 1954, and it wasn't until 1961
that the resources existed to separate the college program from it. The
U-U merger provided the occasion for the break .

It was decided that an Office of College Centers would be created
within the new U.U.A. structure. It would amalgamate the functions of
the College Centers Committee and the Channing-Murray program. By 1961
some $14,000 out of the L.R.Y. budget was being spent on Channing-Murray.
The new College Centers Office appropriated $11,500.00 of that for its
new separate budget.

The question remained as to what kind of gorup the college age
people wished to create. Many of the older L.R.Y. leaders of that time,
such as Jerry Lewis, Mary Van Wilkins, and Gregg Wood, were all interested
in working towards a college students group. A plebiscite of college age
people within L.R.Y. was held to see if there was any support for the idea.

It was decided to hold a separate college conference in the summer of
1961 in the Midwest region. It was the first continental college conference

to be held since the resurgence of college age activity in 1947. The conference voted on September 9, 1961 to constitute themselves as Student Religious Liberals (S.R.L.). Gregg Wood was elected as its first chairman.

S.R.L. was a small organization to start with. In spite of the fact that by 1963 there were seventeen regional College Centers Committees serving over one hundred campus groups, just over one-third of these groups were in touch with S.R.L. The organization functioned independently of, but in relationship with, Orloff Miller and his office.

S.R.L.'s major programs for campus groups in the Sixties consisted of a regular S.R.L. newsletter, the "To:SRL" Packet which they put out to all member groups in co-operation with the Office of College Centers, and the annual Continental Conference. In addition to this, there was S.R.L.'s sponsorship of The Liberal Context, and the European Study Tours in co-operation with the Office of College Centers.

The Liberal Context actually pre-dated S.R.L. In 1960, the College Centers Committee approached L.R.Y.'s Channing-Murray Committee concerning a possible joint publishing venture. The result was a high quality glossy magazine of scholarly articles, journalism, poetry, and reviews. The first editor was Dave Cudhea, who had been one of the people responsible for U.Y.F.'s quality publications in the 1940's. The Liberal Context in its magazine format was the best publication ever to be associated with the U-U youth movement. The depth and diversity of its content rivalled that of the U.U.A.'s Register-Leader on many occasions.

S.R.L. also took over major responsibility for international contacts, since I.R.F. was largely composed of people older than high school age. This created some difficulties at first, particularly when the European

Study Tours were begun. In 1962, the I.R.F. held its conference jointly with S.R.L. in Springfield, Massachusetts. Another extensive automobile tour was co-ordinated by David Gilmartin and Spencer Lavan, and forty I.R.F.ers participated.

The following year it was decided to organize the American trip to Europe for the Dutch I.R.F. Conference, and this developed into a series of summer study tours each year for four following years. One of them included the Soviet Union in its itinerary. The problem between S.R.L. and L.R.Y. at the beginning was whether high school students would be eligible to go. Eventually it was decided that graduating high school seniors could participate. People had to apply for the tours, for they became a popular program.

Right from the beginning of S.R.L., an internal contradiction as to its goals and self-definition was apparent. A 1964 statement on the "Concerns and Objectives" of S.R.L. read in part:

> The most basic personal problem faced by this organi-
> zation is the co-ordination of an ultimately personal
> search with a program of continental and local group
> organization. How can we serve the personal concerns
> of liberal religious students without perverting
> those concerns through the institutional process?

This perceived contradiction would eventually wear S.R.L. down to institutional irrelevence.

Leon Hopper Leaves

The year 1962-63 was the first full year of L.R.Y.'s operation under the new by-laws as a completely high school organization. Maria Fleming was L.R.Y.'s president for that year. It was a disappointing one in many ways for Leon Hopper.

He had high hopes for the new relationship between L.R.Y. and the U.U.A. Particularly, he hoped that the closer structural relationship with the U.U.A., the growth L.R.Y. had undergone, and the new sense of involvement with the denomination among youth would promote greater financial support for youth programs on the denominational level.

However, it soon became apparent that there would be no increases in financial support from the denomination. New programs were being started with Development Fund money but L.R.Y. was not on the priority list for any increases. So Hopper began to look for churches, and in May 1963, he was called to the pulpit in Golden, Colorado. He submitted his resignation to the L.R.Y. Board effective August 31, 1963.

In his final report to the L.R.Y. Board, Leon Hopper expressed a certain ambivalence about the concept of "youth autonomy" in L.R.Y. and how it was expressed in practice. He wanted to reduce the paranoia in youth-adult relations, and as he left office was beginning to see leadership training programs for both youth and adults as an important step in that direction. (One of the last programs he led was an L.R.Y. Advisors' Workshop held in Chicago in May, 1963.)

Hopper also emphasized the importance of field work. He did a considerable amount of travelling in his term of office, to the point where travelling became a central aspect of the L.R.Y. staff job description.

Finally, Hopper reflected upon the growth in L.R.Y. since 1957. He expressed the hope that there could be more depth in conference programming, moving beyond just social getting together. His disappointment at the lack of support from the U.U.A. in the face of a very vital program was quite apparent.

Six years is the longest period of time anyone has stayed on as staff for L.R.Y. The Fifties and early-Sixties represented a period of relative stability compared to the upheaval that was to take place in the next ten years.

SPENCER LAVAN REMEMBERS ALL SOULS, NEW YORK - 1953

For me, LRY was as much a political awakening as a source for
religious inspiration. 1953 was a turning point for me as I completed
the spring of my sophomore year at a conservative Episcopal prep school
in New York. My family attended All Souls Unitarian church, near our
home, where I had been active since second grade. All Souls was then
one of the most Christian and conservative of our churches. Its membership was largely conservative in politics as well.

I had always been a gadfly. The previous year I had been the only
student in my class at school to show interest in Adlai Stevenson months
before his surprise nomination for the Presidency. My belief in his
idealism, his desire to defuse the cold war, his sharp articulation of
what America should be, all motivated my being, setting me apart from
my parents and most of my peers, not to mention my church. The Eisenhower-
Nixon mentality had seized most people around me and I saw them as people
who wanted to hold on to the world as they saw it.

It is hard to remember exactly when we started a youth group at the
church but I do remember it survived largely because of the effective
leadership of Susannah Wilder (Heinz), a new religious education director.
Unlike youth groups in homogeneous suburban or rural towns, we were a
disparate lot coming from schools all over the city and having little in
common other than that our families attended the church.

While we were in part a "confirmation class" who joined the church
in a memorable formal ceremony in the spring of 1954, we were also a
social group and held short worship services at the close of our meetings.
Seeing that we could not survive on individual Sunday meetings alone.
Sue Wilder took some us out where there were other youth, some of whom

had convictions similar to my own. This was the first time I really got
to know another minister in a personal way. In this case it was Vincent
Silliman, our great hymnologist, who touched another important nerve in
my being -- my love for church music.

But a few months later an even more important event took place.
At a conference in Montclair, New Jersey, my first overnight LRY meeting,
Donald Harrington of Community Church delivered a vigorous address on
the need to cease nuclear testing. I had never heard such an outspoken
position taken on an issue that concerned me so deeply. I probably
thought him too radical, if anything, and it would be four years until
I discovered some of the far more radical views of our California religous
liberals.

The effect of these two conferences began to overshadow the significance of the local youth group for me as I moved towards graduation
in 1955. At last I had found a greater community, one outside home
and school with which I could identify. I didn't need to go to extremes
in making my shift. LRY accepted me as I was and I grew greatly in LRY.
In the summer of 1954 I attended the first merged continental LRY
convention in Connecticut and after that every convention as well as
the 1955 and 1956 IRF European tours, until I completed my term as
continental president in 1959.

JEREMY TAYLOR REMEMBERS L.R.Y. + S.R.L. - 1959 - 69

Cold Buffalo (N.Y.)

A difficult place for weathering

Hot desires or honest intellect.

But Channing Club

(Sometimes derived from the verb

"to Chan" - a pun on changing,

Chanting, being serious and close

And honest, & denouncing all

Adult hypocricy)

Was a magic circle

Full of light, and love,

And the aches of hearts

That grew like weeds -

A fountain

Where nourishment was possible

In the midst of the desert.

We ran the show ourselves.

(Even at the time, that was the most

Important thing)

And spoke our righteous indignation

To everyone (especially

Paul Carnes, preaching at him

From his own pulpit).

Our adult advisors practiced

The toleration they preached

(For the most part),

Much to our continuing suprise

And loving consternation.

"The Fed" and conferences

Punctuated our seasons of hot growth

With international friendships

(Some still vital, growing, and among the best

Of adult efforts to be ourselves in company)

And all that good talk

(Impossible to get

With even your closest friends at school

Because of their obedience

To what their parents said was God).

And we ran the show ourselves.

Even at the time, that was the most

Important thing.

"Continental" was a mythic story

Until I went myself and lived the tribal gatherings

From around the world,

(I.A.R.F. always sent older kids-

Young men and women who were not as

Articulately pioneering,

But sharing in our nervous passions none the less).

Turning it into myth while it was happening

With the intensity of our sharing.

And we ran the show ourselves.

Even at the time, that was the most

Important thing.

SRL was fun. (We were legal

Adults now, so, of course we ran the show ourselves.)

But we worked so hard,

And there were so few of us,

We began to get tired of each other's stories

Of how damned hard it was

To put an end to that damned war.

("The Denomination" only sold us out in little ways

And our hearts were never truely broken.)

New generations have new dramas

(Endless variations on the ancient archetypes

Of struggle with the mysteries of being human).

The LRYers I meet now

Are confused about the horrors

We adults continue to practice on the world,

Upon each other and ourselves,

But on the whole they are more polite

In their refusal to believe our words

Are more important than what we are

Than I remember being.

In the on-the-job training

For adult hassles of world stewardship

And adult joys of self-expression,

The best we can do for younger folks (and for ourselves)

Is offer money and good counsel,

No strings attached between the two,

Remembering the deepest values

Of our own experience.

Chapter 8: THE YOUTH AGENDA

Peter Baldwin entered abruptly into the world of L.R.Y. in 1963.
He was serving as a chaplain to U-U students and faculty at the Massachusetts
Institute of Technology when Leon Hopper resigned as Executive Director
of L.R.Y. Baldwin had been a Federation Advisor in New England, and was
available to serve as an interim Executive Director while a permanent one
was being sought. His first Continental Conference was supposed to be a
low-key affair, where he would be testing the water. However, Leon Hopper
came down with appendicitus that week, and Baldwin found himself in the
position of being an instant Executive Director in the midst of what he
has described as "an exceedingly efficient super-organization."

From "Autonomous Youth" to "Vanguard in Progress"

It is convenient to think about L.R.Y. history before 1969 in the
blocks of time marked off by Executive Directors' terms of office. However,
that convenience devalues the importance of the L.R.Y. leadership during
both Hopper's and Baldwin's tenure. Both had a series of competent, dis-
ciplined, and enthusiastic executive committees and boards to work with.
A longer history could more easily focus on each of them without picking
favorites.

The quality of the youth leadership was particularly strong and
particularly important in the transition years after the U-U merger with
Hopper's resignation and Peter Baldwin just beginning his job. L.R.Y.
was a high school age organization for the first time, and there was a
great deal of excitement about that. There was an equal amount of fear
about the degree of control that the adult church would try to exert on
L.R.Y. through the Division of Education.

The L.R.Y. executive committees of the early Sixties had a clear
perspective on what L.R.Y. was and could be. They understood and practised
an institutional discipline which firmly established L.R.Y.'s own unique
space within the denominational structure. The slogan "youth autonomy"
was not only developed as a theoretical ideology during that time. It
was practised responsibily and throughly.

Perhaps part of the reason for the impressive quality of that group
of early Sixties executive committees was that they were to some extent an
oligarchy, i.e. a government by a self-selected few. People were "picked"
early and groomed for L.R.Y. leadership, often moving onto the board and
into the executive committee very predictably. The vice-president or
perhaps a director would almost certainly be the next president. It was
not as devious as it sounds, for these individuals were usually college
sophomores during their final year in L.R.Y. They had been around a long
time, and were logical choices. This situation also provided for more
continuity than exists today, for a person would regularly have served
one year on the continental executive committee before becoming president.

Maria Fleming (L.R.Y. president from 1962-63) was particularly important in seeing that the new L.R.Y. organization was efficiently structured
and effectively working. Her firm style of chairing board meetings might
be frowned upon by L.R.Y.'ers today, but it was a valuable factor in getting
the new high school age board and executive committee into high gear.

Chuck Forrester, L.R.Y.'s president from 1963-64 supported the concept
of "youth autonomy" articulated by Maria Fleming,[1] and strongly believed
that to make that freedom meaningful, L.R.Y. had to have top-notch programs
coming out of its continental office that were directed at the local groups.
The local group was the center of L.R.Y., and federation, regional, and
continental activities should serve and relate directly to the local situations.

The first result of this commitment to locally-directed programs was the L.R.Y. program packet, field-tested and published in the spring of 1964. Peter Baldwin worked through 1963-64 on the creation of a group assessment guide, which was designed to facilitate a local group in evaluating and reaching its potential as a group. Fritz West, a director on that year's committee, began work on a creative worship pamphlet, which came out during his year as L.R.Y. president, succeeding Forrester. Blair Dean, another director on the committee, mercifully laid the ailing L.R.Y. publication, The Youth Leader, to rest, and began in its place The Promethean, a higher quality literary journal, and one of the better publications of L.R.Y. Finally, "Ministry to Youth", the first of three insightful essays by Peter Baldwin about L.R.Y. within the U-U movement, was published. It was an exciting and productive year.

Baldwin was on staff on an interim basis that year, but his style and competence were such that the executive committee recommended that he be hired on a permanent basis. The protege system of executive elections was also brought under control as Chuck Forrester's term ended, although the vice-presidents continued to be elected as presidents for the next three years.

During 1964-65, and 1965-66, the continental office continued the high standards of local programming that had been set by earlier committees. Monthly local group program and information packets were sent out, new program booklets were developed, and two more essays by Peter Baldwin on youth-adult relations appeared.

There was a concern developing among L.R.Y. leaders for more "service projects". The political climate was heating up, youth culture was becoming a more self-conscious entity, and L.R.Y.'s role within the Unitarian Universalist denomination was under examination. Fritz West, president in 1964-65, in his final report, expanded the ideology of youth autonomy to a critique of the denomination, calling for L.R.Y. to see itself as a "vanguard" in the liberal movement:

> Although our heritage and our fundamental values
> derive from the Unitarian Universalist ethos, the
> adults and the youth have formed from that heritage
> different ideologies and religious perspectives. I
> have found that L.R.Y.'ers across the continent are
> uncomfortable with much that the denomination repre-
> sents; its rationalism, its lack of symbolism, its
> relevance to the lives of L.R.Y.'ers. By the mere
> fact of our dissatisfaction, we have a role to play.
> The role of a catalyst, an agitator, and perhaps,
> even a vanguard. Too often L.R.Y.'ers view the
> denomination with disdain, rejecting it as having
> no meaning and searching elsewhere for the warmth
> and worth they found in L.R.Y. What these people
> fail to see is that the ingredients for such an
> experience and such a religion can be found nowhere
> else but in the Unitarian Universalist Association.
> L.R.Y. has a religious approach to offer our denom-
> ination. Its non-rational religious approach, its
> modes of creative worship and its perceptions of the
> religious importance of social action all are a part
> of the challenge.[2]

The thoughts and feelings represented in this statement were to crystallize around various programs and dreams over the next five years.

One was the 1966 Continental Conference, which took as its theme "A
Radical Look at Liberal Religion".

There was a great deal of exciting energy just being tapped within
L.R.Y. in 1964-66. The human potential movement was growing up and out
in small experiments all over the country, and L.R.Y. was one of the
testing grounds for such experiments. Peter Baldwin, working with the
Boston University Human Relations Center, developed designs for structured intergenerational encounters and began training professional group
workers to staff L.R.Y. conferences.

There were rumors from the West Coast of a growing drug scene among
young white people, which some L.R.Y. leaders worried would spell the
doom of their organization. L.R.Y.'ers became more open about their
sexuality, and more adamant in acting out the differences they perceived
their culture and world and that of the adults.

Bill Sinkford, L.R.Y. president in 1965-66, put together a survey
research instrument for us in local groups to get some sense of where
L.R.Y.'ers sexual attitudes and values were moving. It became known as
the Sinkford Sex Survey. Besides providing data for L.R.Y.'s continental
leadership, it proved to be a great icebreaker for local group programming
around sexuality. Leadership training conferences held at summer camps
used various T-group techniques, particularly marathons, to great effect-
iveness.

The mood of L.R.Y. in 1966 when Peter Baldwin was offered a teaching
job at Crane Theological School was confident and strong. In his final
report to L.R.Y., Baldwin recommended an ambitious ten-year program of
fund-raising for the support of four new professional L.R.Y. field workers.
The board accepted a toned-down version of the plan, and called it "Vanguard
in Progress" (V.I.P). The inevitability of the U.U.A.'s financial decline

had not yet become apparent. The Vietnam war was just starting to heat up, but large-scale draft resistance was still a year off. To use Peter Baldwin's phrase, it was "before the lid blew off the culture".

Movement Politics in S.R.L.

The Unitarian Universalist youth movements involvement in the politics of the 1960's is easier to see within S.R.L.'s concerns than in the L.R.Y. program. L.R.Y. printed social responsibility materials and packets for local groups, of course, and political involvement was part of the regular litany of exhortation that L.R.Y.'ers heard out of the Continental office. However, L.R.Y. didn't have a director with primary responsibility for social responsibility until 1967. S.R.L. people were older and were on the campuses. They found themselves in the middle of the civil rights movement and involved in the beginnings of the anti-war movement.

At the occasion of the inauguration of the U.U.A. Department of Social Responsibility, the S.R.L. newsletter quotes a message from Homer Jack, the Director of that office:

"I look forward to working closely with S.R.L. members and groups across the continent. Our Freedom Fund has bailed out several S.R.L. members..."

Through the U.U.A. Freedom Fund a number of S.R.L. members were able to become civil rights workers in the South during the voter registration campaigns.

In the spring of 1965, the entire Unitarian Universalist movement was mobilized, and then shocked, by the march in Selma, Alabama. A U.U. minister, James Reeb, was beaten to death on the street in Selma. His companions at the time were Orloff Miller, of the College Centers Office, and Clark Olson of Berkeley, California. Their accounts of the slaying filled the pages of <u>The Liberal Context</u>.

This event and the beginning of the Free Speech Movement on the Berkeley campus greatly politicized many S.R.L. groups. They organized Free Speech Movements on their own campuses, and the S.R.L. newsletter and <u>The Liberal Context</u> carried articles and news coverage about them.

The S.R.L. Board passed a resolution condemning the war in Vietnam in November, 1965, and entered into a program of co-operation with the Students for a Democratic Society. On many campuses S.D.S. was not allowed to organize, but an S.R.L. group could exist, and S.D.S. was able to function behind the skirts of S.R.L.on a number of campuses.

In 1967-68, the person who had been S.R.L.'s Social Responsibility Chairman throughout much of this period, Michael Ferber, was indicted with Dr. Benjamin Spock and others for conspiracy to resist the draft, arising out of a service at the Arlington Street Church in which draft cards had been turned in and burned. Draft resistance was a major political focus of S.R.L. and continued to be an overriding concern after Ferber's trial and acquital.

The L.R.Y. of The Sixties

I think it is important at this time to take a look at whether the L.R.Y. scene in the Sixties was really any different from the L.R.Y. and A.U.Y.-U.Y.F. groups that preceded it, in order to understand better why events after Peter Baldwin's departure moved as they did. So many of the most significant characteristics of our youth movement appear to me as constant patterns over the years: the intensity of interpersonal relationships; the ambivalent relationship with the denomination; the gap between the continental experience and local group realities; the radical critique of the quality of religious community within our churches;

the role of L.R.Y. as a laboratory for young people to experiment with
who they are.

Are L.R.Y. board meetings any more harrowing to be a part of today
than were the first L.R.Y. council meetings of the early Fifties? Was
there more furor, personal and institutional, around the youth agenda
of 1969 than there was around the W.F.D.Y. issue in 1948? Is the sexual
expression of L.R.Y.'ers any less of an issue than it was in the Forties?
No, I think not. The dynamics of these situations form analogous patterns.
However, there are some differences about the L.R.Y. of the Sixties that
are important to note.

Between 1960 and 1970 all the war babies made their turbulent passage
through adolescence. There were a great many young people around, in L.R.Y.,
and everywhere else, and they were very noticeable. They were a self-
conscious group of young people, even before the media splash of the
later Sixties. I would ascribe some of this self-consciousness to the
fact that they were being defined for the first time in the late Fifties
and early Sixties as a market. A whole world of places and things were
created by the marketing media that were just for them. However, the
media was responding to a developing youth culture as much as it was
creating it.

The significance of L.R.Y.'s becoming a high school organization in
1961 cannot be underestimated here. Even though the age of leadership
was down to the nineteen to twenty-one year range already, this was a
change that made a difference in the way L.R.Y.'ers viewed themselves,
and the way the denomination related to them.

Finally, from a broader sociological point of view, L.R.Y. was an
organization in the right place at the right time, insofar as the cultural

changes of the mid-sixties were concerned. L.R.Y. represented a most
unique institution within the high-school aged community. In many parts
of the continent, L.R.Y. was the only peer group institution unrelated
to all-pervasive social reality of high school that was not organizationally or psychologically dominated by adults. This is possibly less
important today than it was in the mid-Sixties because the cocoon of the
high school world has worn thin in more places today.

However, for many people in high schools in the Sixties, there was
nothing even remotely like L.R.Y. in an otherwise oppressive social
reality. The communications network that L.R.Y. represented, its regional
and continental conferences, were all vehicles that led people out of
that high school and home town cocoon at an earlier age. So when "the
lid blew off the culture", L.R.Y. was one of the pressure points where
the steam first began to burst through.

Staff Changes

Peter Baldwin's departure in 1966 was a blow to L.R.Y. With younger
leadership and less continuity on the executive committee, Baldwin's role
as a permanent administrator as well as a counselor and group leader were
sorely missed. The L.R.Y. board of 1966 voted him in as a life member of
their appreciation.

Ruth Wahtera's executive committee of 1966-67 held the fort while
a new Executive Director was being sought. The job they undertook
was considerable for local and federation activity was at a real peak.
Most of the Wahtera committee was in college and only a few were actually
in Boston. High quality local group packets continued to come out
monthly while a personnel committee sought applications for Executive
Director.

Early in 1967, Richard Earl Kossow was appointed to the job. Instead of a minister or an old L.R.Y.'er, the personnel committee had selected a federation advisor from Minnesota whose profession was law. Kossow was a strong personality in the Boston office, but he had a tremendous amount of faith in the chaotic process of the L.R.Y. leadership experience. He was supportive of the directions the L.R.Y.'ers in the office wanted to take. His skills and interests centered more in the field in the conference situation than in the administrative area. Unfortunately, this was also true of many of the L.R.Y. leaders Kossow worked with.

S.R.L. also went through some staff changes at this time. Orloff Miller resigned from the office of College Centers in 1966 to return to the parish ministry. He was succeeded by Ralph H. (Ron) Cook. Cook became the Executive Director of S.R.L., adopting the pattern of staff relationship which L.R.Y. used. The chair of the S.R.L. board(who at this time was R. Michael McKinlay) worked closely with Cook, for his time had to be split between the field and the office. S.R.L.'s local chapters were always stronger than the continental group ever was. Institutionally, S.R.L. continued to be concerned with how to make itself more representative and how best to deal with the requirements of being the Unitarian-Universalist program for college students.

The Oxford Drug Crisis

The 1967 Continental Conference in Oxford, Ohio seems to mark a kind of turning point in L.R.Y. Youth fares on domestic airlines had just been instituted, so it was a large conference, and a tightly-structured one. It stands out because drugs became a public issue for the first time at a Continental Conference.

The resolution of that drug crisis was a powerful experience for all

concerned. There was wild marijuana growing all over the campus where
the conference was held, and a small group of conferees became joyfully
aware of that fact. At an early meeting of the whole conference, it was
urged that no one harvest the marijuana, let alone smoke any of it. At
the end of the week, four conferees were caught smoking. Greg Sweigert
had just been elected the new president of L.R.Y. in an emotionally-
charged election, and this was his baptism of fire.

A long conference of L.R.Y. leaders, advisors, and the busted L.R.Y.'ers
was held. Finally it was decided to bring the whole matter up for the
entire conference to talk about. It was the last night of what had been
a great conference. Bob Dylan's "Like a Rolling Stone" had screamed
underneath the surface of the 1966 Continental Conference, but his was
the summer of "Sgt. Pepper's Lonely Hearts Club Band". The air was full
of stories of a wonderful renaissance happening among young people all
over the country. How could a few L.R.Y.'ers possibly shatter that
feeling by explicitly doing something that they had been told would
threaten the very existence of L.R.Y. as an organization? It was hard
to reconcile.

The conference gathering wallowed in the contradictions and ambivalent
feelings for a long time. Finally, it was decided that the culprits would
not be turned over to any authorities, and it was too late in the conference
to ask them to leave. They would instead be asked to write a letter to
the L.R.Y. Board reflecting on why they had decided getting high at this
conference was so important. A healing process had begun through all
this, but things were never quite the same afterwards. Similar problems,
and wider issues concerning the style of the American presence within
the I.R.F., plagued the I.R.F. Conference which was held in Stanstead,
Quebec that same summer. The drug issue continues to flare up in similar

ways today.

A "W.C. Fields" Trip

At the 1967 board meetings Dick Kossow outlined clearly to the
L.R.Y. board the kind of financial crisis the U.U.A. was facing. The
board took a hard look at the Vanguard in Progress program, for it seemed
apparent that the U.U.A. would not be able to match any money that L.R.Y.
raised through it. It was decided in a burst of denominational enthusiasm
to change the V.I.P program to a fund-raising effort for the U.U.A. When
it came time to choose a   for the program, everyone looked over Greg
Sweigert's head to the poster that had hung behind him all meeting;
W.C. Fields peering over a stacked poker hand. So began the W.C. Fields
Tripping program, which managed to raise $5,000 from L.R.Y. local groups
in one year for the U.U.A. annual fund.

The people attending the 1967 Continental Conference and board
meetings carried a great deal back to their federations and locals.
The Sweigert committee travelled extensively, and sent out posters,
packets, and copies of The Promethean edited by Ken Friedman.[3] The degree
of involvement the locals felt was reflected in the amount of money they
raised for the W.C. Fields fund. Sweigert was to present the cheque for
$5,000 to U.U.A. president Dana Greeley with much ceremony at the 1968
General Assembly in Cleveland. Unfortunately, Sweigert forgot the cheque
in Boston, so when he ambled up on the platform to get the famous Greeley
handshake, he was clutching in his hand an envelope containing only an
I.O.U.

L.R.Y. attempted its first major political organizing within the
denomination at the 1968 General Assembly. The Denver Assembly in 1967
had seen but a smattering of L.R.Y.'ers largely because of its awkward

timing (late May) when everyone was still in high school. There were
nearly thirty L.R.Y.'ers in Cleveland in 1968 when the Black Affairs
Council controversy surfaced in the denomination. The L.R.Y. delegates
mostly favored the one million dollar budget allotment over four years
that the B.A.C. was asking for (a figure based on one dollar per year
per Unitarian Universalist). The role that L.R.Y. took at that Assembly
was that of peacemaker and court jester. They waved "Dana loves Hayward"
signs in the middle of tense debates on the Assembly floor.[4]

L.R.Y. had developed on overt "hippie" image in the denomination
by now. When Larry Ladd was running for president of L.R.Y. in 1968,
he grew his beard out in order to look more hip. In spite of Larry's
"straight" reputation, he was elected at the Santa Fe, New Mexico Continental Conference. The theme of that Continental Conference centered
around marathon group work. The whole conference divided into cell groups
led by one adult and one youth facilitator. The groups met together for
the first part of the conference, and the remainder of the week was built
out of that experience. Similar kinds of themes had been happening in
other L.R.Y. conferences and camps elsewhere that year; in particular, at
the Lake Geneva, Wisconsin conference held before Continental. A close
and powerful group of L.R.Y.'ers emerged out of that conference experience,
and burst onto the Continental L.R.Y. scene over the next three years,
electing six executive committee members during that period.

During the following autumn another style of conference programming
emerged. The prototype conference was held in Toronto in the fall of 1968.
Its theme (or non-theme) was "Do Your Own Schtick", and it began a trend
of non-thematic conferences centered around individual workshops on a
wide variety of topics. People from all over the East and the Mid-west

attended the "Schtick Conference", even though it was supposed to be an Eastern Canada Federation conference.

The Larry Ladd Executive Committee was a diverse combination of people. Ladd himself was a calm systematic administrator. The committee also included two full-time field trippers, a Social Actions Director, and the youngest person ever elected to an L.R.Y. executive committee position (Deborah Mendelsohn, age 16). The L.R.Y. board also commissioned Greg Sweigert to stay in Boston to edit a new L.R.Y. publication to replace the expensive and ailing Promethean. It was to be called The Nameless Newsprint. So with Richard Kossow on full-time, the Boston office had three to five staff people on hand and two to four people in the field all year.

The 1968 board meetings, the last to be held in the pattern established by the Council of the Fifties, was held in August in the New Mexican desert. The board members were deeply affected by concern for the people that had left Continental Conference the week before to go join the demonstrations in Chicago against the Democratic Party National Convention.

The Youth Agenda

The year 1968-69 was a crucial one for L.R.Y. The organization's character was changing dramatically from the bottom up. The locals of 1968 were dealing with all the new issues that "youth culture" had formed around: drug use, the human potential movement, music, a new sexual ethic, the draft, the war. The L.R.Y. executive committee had a more noticeable physical presence at the Boston office, day and night, feeling like they were in the eye of a hurricane and not quite sure in which direction to go.

The Nameless Newsprint became a major communication link between Boston and the locals. The committee of 1968-69 began the year working mostly

with L.R.Y. locals and federations, but as the year wore on U.U.A. politics

began to absorb more and more of their energy. Furthermore, it was becoming

apparent that Richard Kossow wouldn't stay on as Executive Director much

longer. Ladd took a much stronger role in the organization and admini-

stration of L.R.Y. during the latter part of the year.

1969 was an intensely political year in the U.U.A., and the L.R.Y.

was in the thick of it. Executive committee members were part of the

"FULLBAC" coalition of white supporters of the Black Affairs Council.

It was clear that B.A.C. funding would be challenged at the General

Assembly in Boston that year. It was a U.U.A. presidential election year,

and most of the candidates were paying attention to the youth presence

within the denomination. In the spring of 1969, Robert Hohler, Executive

Director of the Layman's League, held a sit-in fast in the lobby of 25

Beacon Street to call attention to the U.U.A.'s investment policies, and

the Unitarian Universalist Service Committee building was occupied by

the Interdenominational Radical Caucus, to protest the U.U.S.C.'s project

work in Vietnam. The I.R.C. drew much support from local L.R.Y.'ers and

S.R.L.'ers in Boston.

While all this was going on, the L.R.Y. leadership was formulating

plans of its own. L.R.Y.'s institutional situation at the time was at

a crossroads. Kossow would be leaving at the year's end. L.R.Y. had

continued to grow in size, even beyond the big growth spurt during Leon

Hopper's years. Yet there had been no funding increase from the U.U.A.

or its predecessors since the time L.R.Y. was formed in 1954. The I.R.Y.

board directly controlled about ten thousand dollars of its own budget,

which it obtained in endowment interest and federation dues. The rest

of the L.R.Y.'s money was held by the Department of Education and paid
out in professional staff salaries, travel and office needs.   The L.R.Y.-
S.R.L. endowment fund was held in the U.U.A.'s General Investment Fund,
and was involved in a number of politically questionable stocks.   The
1968-69 committee had more full-time L.R.Y.'ers than ever before, and
they felt much closer to the program needs of the L.R.Y.'ers they knew.
It seemed worth the risk to try to gain full control of L.R.Y.'s financial
resources and build a totally youth-run program.

Larry Ladd laid out the philosophy behind L.R.Y.'s new political
stance in an article in the Nameless Newsprint entitled "Bitter Brooklyn."
It was a far-reaching statement which outlined the liberation issues
high school students in general were dealing with.   In April, 1969, in
Huntington, Long Island, a meeting of the 1968-69 executive committee
and all the candidates nominated or running for office in 1969 was held
to formulate a Youth Agenda for General Assembly.

It was decided that a major effort at getting youth delegates to
General Assembly would be mounted.   L.R.Y. would be demanding U.U.A.
funding of $100,000 for youth programs and complete control of their own
endowment fund.   They decided not to hire another Executive Director.
To save money on board meetings and to help get people to the General
Assembly, it was decided to hold the continental board meetings immediately
after General Assembly instead of at the Continental Conference later
that summer.

It was an embattled U.U.A. administration that received the demands.
The reaction in the churches went all the way from disbelief and hostility
through cautious support to boredom.

In the end a compromise was reached before the issue got to the G.A.

floor. Raymond Hopkins, the U.U.A. vice president, did a cost-accounting study of L.R.Y. and S.R.L. and pointed out that there was nearly $100,000 being spent annually on the two programs already, counting in all staff salaries, expenses, office costs, rent for the office at 25 Beacon Street and the Billings Lecture Fund which S.R.L. was controlling and using to send Ric Masten, the U-U troubador or minister, around the country. Hopkins offered to remove L.R.Y. and S.R.L. from the Department of Education budget, grant them their money directly, and release the endowment from the General Investment fund, if both organizations would pay the U.U.A. directly for all the services they used. The L.R.Y.'ers agreed. S.R.L. did too, but more cautiously. Ron Cook was also resigning his position to go to Starr King School as a member of the faculty, so S.R.L. was in the same position as L.R.Y.

The Youth Agenda was therefore resolved to some extent even before the General Assembly began. However, the momentum that had been built up was applied to the rest of the business before the Assembly. About one hundred young people participated in the 1969 G.A. Some sixty-two were delegates. The young people and the I.R.C. group established a small encampment on the mezzanine floor of the Statler Hilton Hotel in Boston. They were hard to miss in their plywood geodesic dome. The youth leadership conducted informational meetings for the youth delegates where representatives of all sides of the issues before the Assembly had a chance to explain their positions, particularly various groups that had formed around the issue of Black Affairs Council funding.

It was suggested by some after the Assembly was over that the youth delegates were somehow set up and manipulated by the B.A.C. people in the events that followed. Actually, they were kept informed of the floor strategy the Black Caucus was planning, and were never overtly pressured into anything. The night before the issue came to a head, the B.A.C. leadership and their L.R.Y.-age members briefed the Youth Caucus leadership on exactly what alternatives were being considered. The L.R.Y. delegates expected a siezure of the microphones to occur, and had been told that the degree to which they supported that action was up to them. Each person who responded by blocking access to the microphones when the Assembly refused to change the Agenda to allow the B.A.C. question to be considered immediately acted out of his or her own conscience.

The walkout when the funding motion was finally defeated was unexpected and spontaneous. Most of the youth delegation decided to walk, many feeling like they were walking out of the denomination altogether. As the day wore on, it became apparent that some common ground upon which the Assembly could get back together had to be found. The Youth Caucus decided to seek that ground in a worship service.

People from all sides of the issue attended the L.R.Y. service that evening after the walkout in the Arlington Street Church. They all joined in singing the L.R.Y. Hymn, "We Would Be One" - twice through - at the end. It wasn't any solution, but it was a beginning. It was important to stay together. When the Fellowship for Renewal people returned to the main Assembly body, L.R.Y.'ers dumped boxes of balloons from the balcony over the heads of the delegates.

When the vote on B.A.C. funding was finally re-considered, the young people voted nearly unanimously in favor of the commitment to B.A.C. The vote was close, but it carried.

The 1969 General Assembly felt like one great public victory for the leaders of the Youth Caucus, but it would be the prelude to a series of small back-room defeats.

LUCIE MEIJER REMEMBERS I.R.F. - 1966-76

What has been important to me about being in the I.R.F.? - First
and most of all learning to accept other people's way of life. Can you
imagine that I was embarassed when an American friend who stayed with me
made himself a super sandwich at my table?   It's not that I couldn't
afford such an expense, but I was brought up in the years of scarcity
just after World War II in the Netherlands, a country that has known many
a hungry winter. Moreover, we are taught to be modest when we are the
guest in another's home. I've known many other situations in which my
childhood - or deeply anchored and culturally determined - convictions
were shaken by friends from other countries.

There also exist all sorts of differences in thinking between the
various language groups. I attended a workshop once on "language" at
a conference, and while the English-speaking people were eager to begin,
a French person asked: "Are we talking about 'langue, language, parole,
or mot?" In other words, the French think in more precise categories
for the concept of language. I've always found it amusing that the
constitution of IRF (published in both English and German)contains the
provision: "in case of doubt, the English version shall rule!" And
English phrases are often so ambigous!

Discovering my own values has been a striking aspect of going to
IRF for me. It has provided an opportunity to build long-lasting relationships. Having been at eleven summer IRF conferences I can testify
that IRF is able to creat a support group for youth and young adults
from many parts of the world.

One thing is certain. I have experienced many firsts in my life
at IRF meetings; I've made my first and only macrame belt, played a

simulation game on world development for the first time, had my first
women's discussion in IRF, enjoyed and felt comfortable in a worship
service as I'd never done before, stayed up to watch the sunrise, ate
my first lobster, stood for the first time in a circle holding many
friends and singing the two following chants that summarize for me
the meaning of the International Religious Fellowship:

wearing my long wing feathers

as I fly

I circle around

the boundaries of the earth

Listen Listen Listen

to my heart's song

I will never forget you

I will never forsake you

ROB ISAACS REMEMBERS CHICAGO 1966 - 69

Attention:

      (but you know that's only part of it)
We had a space that was ours only.
enlightening leaded windows, grey stone walls
a pervasive solidity, cool and comfortable.
We painted it black.

The Skunch Room:

      Where-in we re-writ All of Us in Wonderland.
Seven levels, to be precise,
all in a room which was probably not larger
than twelve by twenty.
Seven levels built from old lumber carried up
from the inner basement.
The room next to the crypt for the Skunch room
rested peacefully and in its racuous moments also,
upon a shadowed catacomb holy and mysterious.

Damn right a place to love and hide !

The shelter of our confessions,
our sanctuary.

It was just the same as this moment then,
only faster. We were so much more desperate
to age.

"There is no such thing as retreat,
there is only strategic withdrawal."
(The R.O.T.C. Handbook)

If we learned to love and hide and recuperate,
we also learned to struggle in the world.

For we have a vision and we are not the only ones.
Out of old lumber and resting upon
the integrity of a common dream,

We have set out to build.

To you who are fearful:
I am fearful also. The awkward dance we danced
so laughable, so exquisite,
searching for balance, learning to rely on breath.
It is not beyond you to sense the ecstasy
as well as the danger.

High drama is worthy of attention.
I tell you the church is the womb.
It is the place of birth and dedication.
It gave us a place to love.
We will be true to its
holy intention.

Chapter 9: THE NEW COMMUNITY?

The L.R.Y. Board of Trustees that met in Concord, Massachusetts,
after the 1969 General Assembly was quite shell-shocked. Besides the
kind of week it had been at G.A., they now had the responsibility of
carving up a $45,000 budget for the first time. Elections were a painful
process, with three positions on the new Executive finally being filled
by appointments, largely of losing candidates. Robert Isaacs was elected
President.

The First Year

The 1969 L.R.Y. Board was feeling its oats, and adopted a strong
"states' rights" position. Rather than pay dues to Continental any more,
they wanted a piece of the new-found wealth for the regional level. The
first budget that was drawn up, based on everyone's stated needs and the
programs the executive committee members had in mind, added up to $62,000.
A process of budget cutting began which continued for years. Half-way
through the year the U.U.A. cut the L.R.Y. budget by nearly one-third,
down to $32,000, as the new U.U.A. president, Robert West, began drastic
surgery on the U.U.A.'s finances. So, much of the work in Concord was
all in vain.

The board met again later that summer in Seabeck, Washington, at
the Continental Conference. More budget squabbling took interminable
time. There was a great deal of alienation between the executive committee and the board as a result of the whole process. The conference
itself was quite successful in contrast to the board meeting. Its theme
was "Stewed Rhubarb". It was the first Continental Conference to operate
on the workshops-only model. There was a beautiful madness surrounding

it. The Sahili Federation executive committee won the prize offered for
the most original arrival at the conference by driving in atop a full-
sized mobile calliope.

At their 1969 Continental Conference in Colorado Springs, Colorado,
Student Religious Liberals went through a significant re-structuring.
Ron Cook had left and no new professional staff person was to be hired.
S.R.L. was beginning to see itself with a wider constituency than just
college students, and wanted to try a budgeting approach that would allow
the constituency maximum opportunity to start locally-based projects on
their own initiative. The organization was renamed S.R.L., A Free Religious
Fellowship, reflecting these changes.

The 1969-70 executive committee was the first to set up shop full-
time with an apartment in Boston. They worked with a hired secretary
and an adult advisor rather than any new Executive Director. By January,
1970, the high hopes and tight organization they tried to put into effect
were crumbling around them. A variety of things contributed to the decay.
The L.R.Y. board had been merciless in their budget allotment for the
committee's personal needs, so they were living in a slum apartment in
Cambridge and making fifty dollars a month. The disagreements with the
board of trustees were a constant grind. When the U.U.A. cut the budget
in November, the group could not agree on how priorities ought to be
realigned. It was discouraging to be around the U.U.A. as well. L.R.Y.
had decided to make as firm a commitment to the Black Affairs Council as
possible beyond mere political support by pledging one-half of their
endowment fund to the B.A.C. Bond program. At the same time, the U.U.A.
administration would recommend and the board would approve that B.A.C.
funding be cut, in spite of the General Assembly votes of 1968 and 1969.

In February, 1970, the Executive Committee members agreed to work independently on their program responsibilities without concensus until summer.

As General Assembly time approached again, the executive committee began pulling itself back together again. L.R.Y.'s General Assembly plans were co-ordinated with the Fellowship for Renewal, which had been created as an on-going organization from the group that walked out of the 1969 G.A. An old hotel in Seattle that was being operated as a hippie hostel was found, and L.R.Y. rented it for $100 for G.A. week. They offered free "crash space" at the"beautiful" Fremont Hotel for anyone who wanted it, and private rooms at a minimal cost. The Seattle press headlined a story about the Unitarian Universalist convention as "A Tale of Two Hotels". The L.R.Y. leadership at that General Assembly spearheaded a drive for passage of resolutions on legalization of marijuana and equal rights for homosexuals, and were successful. They also got a commitment that every effort would be made to have General Assemblies in late June to allow people in school to attend.

In so many ways the Youth Agenda goals that had been set for 1968-70 had been fulfilled, but that satisfaction was embittered by the constant threat of continuing budget cuts and uncertainty among L.R.Y.'s leadership as to direction.

Looking for the New Community

L.R.Y. since 1970 has gone through a trial and error process of finding the best way to function under its own leadership and within the precarious new relationship with the U.U.A. The change in 1969 was a major one, and it was a full three years before organizational roles and patterns were established that could provide some degree of stability and efficiency within the leadership. The 1970-71 committee, with Larry Brown as President, fragmented as badly as the one before it. The eight member committee was too top-heavy. Four members were asked to resign at mid-year to bring the leadership down to a manageable and responsible group.

In the fall of 1970, the U.U.A. decided to establish a committee of their board to act as a funnel for the Youth Program monies. Leon Hopper, at that time a member of the U.U.A. board, was appointed as a representative to this new Youth Adult committee along with Julie Underwood. Since then a long process of trust-building has gone on in order to approach an effective working relationship. The Youth Adult Committee gradually developed from being a Board watchdog committee into a valuable advisory body for U-U youth programming.

In 1971, Charles B. (Chuck) Rosene was elected president of a four-person Executive Committee. Serving with him were Molly Monahan, Kim Yasutake, and Rick Reiser. This committee established itself in a relatively stable living situation, and began to function in a more productive collective fashion than its two predecessors had ever been able to manage.

They decided to remain Boston-based and to try to bring L.R.Y.'s focus back to relevant programming for local groups. The L.R.Y. office was re-organized and mutually satisfactory diplomatic relations with the denomination were restored.

The task that this committee and the ones that have succeeded it have undertaken is to try to move with the changes that have taken place in high-school age culture as reflected in L.R.Y. local groups. Developing programmatic materials for high school students remains as problematic as it ever has been, perhaps even more so.

The first step in this direction consisted of re-cycling the old 1960's L.R.Y. programs. They were reprinted, adapted, or completely rewritten to fit the needs of the L.R.Y.'ers of today.

The New Community was a program approach designed by the 1972-73 executive committee of Gale Pingel, Claudia Nalven, Holly Horn, and John Byrne. It offered a wide range of program suggestions for L.R.Y. local groups which were designed to help them develop an image of themselves as a caring, extended family with its base in a concept of religious community which furthers personal liberation. The program took advantage of the skills and approaches to adult programming within the U.U.A. Department of Education, and it was based on a vision of what a meaningful L.R.Y. local group could be. It furthermore incorporated a badly-needed feminist perspective which was lacking in L.R.Y. programming before that time.

This executive committee decided to abandon a heirarchical model of leadership structure which they saw as inconsistent with their political philosophy. So Gale Pingel became the last president of L.R.Y. When the 1972-73 committee retired, a new system of directorships was established. Each executive committee member was to be elected to a position with a specific job description. The committee attempts to make broad policy decisions on a collective basis.

A People Soup

The 1973-74 executive committee (Adam Auster, Peter Nalven, Paula Rose, and Matthew Easton) managed to re-do the constitution and by-laws to reflect the changing character of L.R.Y. Their major innovation in programming was to initiate People Soup, a newspaper which was to be mailed directly up to eight times a year to all L.R.Y. members. This was the first consistent program publication to come out of L.R.Y. since the Nameless Newsprint folded in 1970. Initially, the committee tried to put People Soup out on a subscription basis, using a special grant

grant from the Youth Adult Committee to support the first few issues.
Beginning in 1974-75 it was mailed free to every Unitarian Universalist
church, a large mailing list of L.R.Y. members, and anyone else who
wanted it. Cream of People Soup was initiated by Bev Treumann in 1975,
in order to compile all the best local group program ideas from several
issues into one paper.

A Youth Caucus within the U.U.A. was created in 1975 under the
leadership of L.R.Y. Director Lara Stahl. The Youth Caucus was intended
to be a rallying point for all U-U youth attending the annual General
Assembly. Although the Youth Caucus was organized by L.R.Y. it effectively served young people within the denomination unaffiliated with
L.R.Y. Through raising scholarship funds and providing information
and discussion sessions about the issues, the caucus began to provide
a valuable home base for all young people finding their way through
the large and often confusing process of G.A.

Almost all the executive committees of the 1970's experienced con-
tinual tension arising from the day-to-day grind of living with the
people you work with. Several changes of apartments, gradually increasing
the available living space for the four executives, temporarily alleviated
difficult situations. However, extra space would all too soon be filled
by the inevitable army of travelling L.R.Y.'ers who would come to stay
for a few hours, a few days, or a few months. The creation in 1976 of
a month-long internship program for L.R.Y.'ers interested in trying out
the executive committee experience added to the apartment crowding.
There were only three executive committees from 1969 to 1979 that survived
their full year term without the resignation of at least one member.

The lack of continuity from one executive committee to another multi-

plied the enormity of the task that the new group arriving in Boston each
fall had to face. The committees involved in this transition in 1974 tried
to remedy this situation by choosing one member of the outgoing group to
stay on in the office into the fall of the new fiscal year to provide
training and consultation for the incoming group. Then, in 1977, the
L.R.Y. Board decided to stagger the Executive Committee terms, electing
two in the winter and two in the summer, in order to maximize the continuity within the leadership.

L.R.Y. In Decline

By the year 1974 it was apparent that Liberal Religious Youth on
the regional and on the local levels was suffering a serious decline.
Some critics were quick to blame the decline in the size and strength
of local programs on the radical youth leadership ideology that was
strongest in 1968-1971. Most districts in the association had one or
more churches that suffered property damage, inconvenience to members,
or other kinds of casualties connected to L.R.Y. events that were completely youth-run and run badly. The ideology of the youth-run program
is identified with the LRY'ers who first became publicly involved with
drug use, unconventional costumes, and greater sexual freedom at younger
ages. Teenagers (and parents) who do not embrace this kind of adolescent lifestyle felt uncomfortable about involving themselves with the
local L.R.Y. group. Some churches tried to remedy this situation by
dropping the name L.R.Y. and setting up youth groups that were led by
adults and insulated from contact with regional and continental L.R.Y.
programs.

There was indeed a fire burning to generate all this smoke. Youth
leadership on the continental level often meant that efficiency and out-

reach of the central office for youth programming within the denomination suffered. This was due partly to the lifestyle and work process that adolescents collectively adopt when they come to Boston for a year to do the job. It was due partly to a lack of expertise on the part of youth leaders with respect to efficient office procedures. It was also due to the fact that Unitarian Universalist church leaders were much less willing to co-operate with and respond to the efforts made by youth leaders to have an influence on local programming.

Factors beyond the control of both youth and adult leaders also played a major part on this decline. A typical member of Liberal Religious Youth in 1974 was born between 1957 and 1959 and entered adolescence in the 1970's. The baby boom wave of young people that had washed over the denomination in the Sixties was clearly over. There were considerably fewer adolescents around to be members of any youth group, whether it called itself L.R.Y. or not.

Youth culture in the 1970's no longer had the sharp focus it did in the late Sixties. What had been frontiers for adolescents five years before were now playgrounds. Politically and sociologically, there seemed to be no clear directions for young people to go in as there had been before.

Unitarian Universalism was also in decline over this same period of years. In addition to fewer adolescent children among church families, there were fewer church families in the 1970's bringing their children up through church school. Many of our churches, especially in urban areas, increasingly became made up of single people. This fact made one phenomenon in some of our churches particularly curious. This was the tendency to regard L.R.Y.'ers whose parents were not Unitarian Universalist as "outsiders" instead of "converts" who were making a connection with the levels of institutional Unitarian Universalism that they could most easily relate to.

With a smaller membership base to draw on, discouraged by the frustration and hostility felt by many adults, and hurt by a lack of leadership skills and motivation passed on from one generation of L.R.Y.'ers to the next, many L.R.Y. regions and federations and locals simply dried up. Our churches were often glad to see them go.

The S.R.L. Land Rush

Whereas L.R.Y. made a relatively successful transition into the mechanics of running its own program, Student Religious Liberals never really did. The role of the S.R.L. Executive Secretary in Boston, Joanne Powers, was reduced to that of a newsletter editor and a channel of communication between board members. The new board members of S.R.L., a Free Religious Fellowship, lost interest in doing the kind of field work and correspondence necessary to keep in touch with their eroding base of campus S.R.L. groups.

In the winter of 1971 the board decided to fire Ms. Powers, and to install one of their own members in Boston as the Executive Secretary. The group also became interested at that time in an idea which would consume the time and energy of three successive "generations" of S.R.L. people all the way to 1977. The idea was to invest the S.R.L. share of the endowment fund for youth programming in land, and establish a community of S.R.L. people who would function as a model for others and who would do the job of co-ordinating the S.R.L. organization. People who got excited about the idea over the years were long on dreams and good intentions, but short on practical know-how and long-term commitment.

The first group that tried to pull together a land investment fell apart due to greed and lack of trust among the board members. The money was mismanaged, and the U.U.A.'s Youth Adult decided to cut the S.R.L. program budget back from $25,000 to a bare institutional minimum of $7,000. A younger group of college age people picked up the pieces and tried to bring the organization back to life. They hired Wayne Arnason, a student at Harvard Divinity School and a former L.R.Y. leader to run their office.

At the 1973 S.R.L. Continental Conference at DeBenneville Pines in California, a new group of S.R.L.'ers caught land fever and began the hunt all over again. This new group looked very throughly at pieces of land in California, Florida, and New England before settling on a property in upstate New York near Saratoga Springs. At the 1974 Continental Conference in Colorado the decision to buy was made, and "pioneers" volunteered or were recruited to be the first to live on the property, and to get it into shape before winter set in. However, when the group met all together on the actual property to seal the deal, they realized the enormity of the task facing them, and decided that they didn't have the stamina to see it through. This group of S.R.L.'ers continued to function for another year, but the collapse of the land plans had destroyed the momentum that the group had generated.

The institutional structure of S.R.L. languished until a new group picked up the pieces agian in 1976. By now the campus groups of S.R.L. had all but vanished, and the group had become an alumni association of old L.R.Y.'ers who wanted to continue the friendships and conference experiences that had been so important for them in L.R.Y.

The next group to take over the S.R.L. structure decided to make explicit the fact that the group was no longer the denomination's college

age program in any real sense. It had become a network of young adults
with varying connections to Unitarian Universalism who were interested
in alternative lifestyles and communal living. They decided to call
themselves Communities for Study and Action (C.S.A.). The C.S.A. group
decided not to ask the U.U.A. for continued funding and proceeded in their
own direction. In the summer of 1978, it was decided to dissolve what
was left of the institutional structure of Student Religious Liberals
and to return the S.R.L. portion of the endowment fund to L.R.Y.

S.R.L.'s story over the past ten years has not been entirely one
of decline and dissolution. For seven summers after the structural
changes of 1969-70, there were annual conferences which drew an average
of seventy-five to one hundred people each. The program continued to
provide a community within Unitarian Universalism for hundreds of young
adults who had been highly motivated by their L.R.Y., experiences but
now found that they had no place to put all that energy. For a smaller
group of people the land projects were an invaluable learning experience.

S.R.L. people became more deeply involved with International Religious
Fellowship during this period because of contacts made early in the
Seventies between L.R.Y. and S.R.L. leaders and I.R.F. people. In 1972,
the S.R.L. and I.R.F. conferences were held jointly on Cape Cod, Massachusetts. The Americans organized and led a two week tour of the Eastern
U.S.A. and Canada before the conference which helped in building friendships and community. In 1975, the Americans did it again, offering their
European friends a three week tour of Western Canada and the U.S.A.,
culminating in a long bus ride back across America to the I.R.F. and S.R.L.
conferences held in Western Massachusetts at summer's end.

With the shutdown of S.R.L.'s operations in 1978, these formal contacts
no longer exist. I.R.F. relied on old friends and L.R.Y. leaders to keep

Americans informed on its programs and activities. The Unitarian Universalist Association no longer has the funds to support an organization
for or a ministry to college age people. A gathering of UU's with
expertise in college programming held in April of 1975 produced no
new directions in this area, and it appears that if they are to arise
they will have to come from the District level.

I.R.F. and the Art of Living Together

International Religious Fellowship continued to thrive in the late
Sixties, although Albert Schweitzer College did not. The college was
moved from Churwalden to a site near Lausanne, Switzerland in 1965,
and I.R.F. lost touch with it after that.[1]

In 1966, I.R.F. became a full member group of the International
Association for Religious Freedom. During the Seventies, as I.A.R.F.
changed from a scholarly conclave to a "world council" of liberal
religious churches, I.R.F. members became much more involved in its
congresses and activities. While there were only a handful of I.R.F.
people at the I.A.R.F. Congress in Heidelburg in 1972, the 1972 Montreal
Congress saw a busload of I.R.F.'ers ride up to participate following
their own conference in Massachusetts. The 1978 I.R.F. Conference was
held in conjunction the I.A.R.F. Congress, and had over sixty young
people in attendence.

In the late Sixties and early Seventies, I.R.F. conference themes
and styles of programming moved away from abstract topics to more
personally oriented themes. This was partly due to the influence of the
American L.R.Y. and S.R.L. members who had become involved in I.R.F.
However, the youth culture of the Sixties was an international phenomenon
and there was a desire within the European member groups to move the

annual conference onto a deeper level. The 1971 conference theme was
"Mind Expansion". The 1973 conference was the scene of fierce controversy
regarding the respect individual I.R.F.'ers awarded religious symbols,
especially Christian religious symbols. The 1974 conference was built
around "The Art of Living Together", with encounter groups and sensitivity
training techniques. In 1975 in America the conference dealt with sexism
in both personal and political terms.

The I.R.F./S.R.L. tours in America cemented many important friendships and offered an opportunity for young religious liberals from Europe
to see America from the inside out. The European group reciprocated with
a 1978 tour of Europe for American friends after the I.R.F.- I.A.R.F.
Congress. The first I.R.F. tour of Japan was held in the summer of 1975.

I.R.F.'s member groups are not as strong today as they have been
in the past. The liberal religious movements in Europe are not large,
and they have experienced the same decline in the involvement of young
adults as the Unitarian Universalist Association. The style in which
the organization survices will depend a great deal on whether I.R.F.
remains an organization of member groups or becomes simply a society
of individual members.

The S.C.O.Y.P. Report

In late 1875 concern grew about the lack of support for youth
programming in the Unitarian Universalist denomination. In 1976 the
members of the Continental L.R.Y. executive committee became acutely
aware of these inadequacies. Acting at the suggestion of L.R.Y., the
U.U.A. Board voted to establish a Special Committee on Youth Programs
(S.C.O.Y.P.) with the following charge:

"...to study the existing youth programs in the denomination,
including L.R.Y., and to make proposals, including budget proposals, to

the Board as to the best ways for the U.U.A. to develop, offer and support programs for youth generally of high school age.

The Board agreed that the budget recommendations of the Committee should include alternatives..."

A committee of seven people, three youth and four adults, was appointed. It included former and current L.R.Y. leaders and advisors, as well as youth and adults active in UU youth programs other than L.R.Y.

The committee held four meetings, and spent over fifteen months compiling information and examining youth programs throughout the Unitarian Universalist denomination.

The committee returned a twenty-five page report in November, 1977.

The general conclusions were reported. The first was that the status quo was inadequate and a disservice to youth. Secondly, that there had been a massive abdication of responsibility by the adult church in regard to youth programming. The report analyzed the reasons for these two problems, and proceeded to make several alternative recommendations for action with projected budgets attached to each one.

The most substantial recommendation was that the resident executive committee of L.R.Y. be replaced by an Office of Youth Programs, staffed by an adult and a secretary. Liberal Religious Youth would continue to be funded for specific kinds of programming but not for the support of their elected leaders in a central office in the U.U.A. structure. The committee also recommended that the denomination's Youth Adult committee to be restructured and that a denomination-wide dialogue be conducted over two years culminating in a funded intergenerational conference on the continental level.

To no one's surprise, the report generated a great deal of contro-

versy. The leaders, members, and friends of liberal religious youth
felt like they had been made the scapegoats for a complex of problems
that had resulted in the decline of the youth program. The common
placebo for all denominational ills, a staff person in an office,
seemed like a particularly tired and inappropriate solution to the
situation. On the other side, many in the denomination felt that some
dramatic action had to be taken to pull the youth program out of the
doldrums, and they could not see the L.R.Y. executive committee or
board becoming an agent for such an action.

The 1977-78 executive committee, consisting of Shelley Cantril
Susan Buis, Abbe Bjorkland, and Barbara Dykes was a particularly
efficient,hard-working committee. Their efforts to rally support
against the S.C.O.Y.P. recommendations resulted in a nine month
moratorium on any decision in order to encourage further response from
the local level.

Churches, L.R.Y. groups, district youth-adult committees and religious
education committees, all held discussions and forums on S.C.O.Y.P.'s
recommendations. Their responses reflected the continuing polarization
within the Unitarian Universalist Association as to whether Liberal
Religious Youth was adequate to continue as the denomination's only
youth program.

Meeting in March of 1979, the continental Youth-Adult committee's
action was similarly polarized. A majority of the committee members
(most of whom were youth)endorsed a recommendation that the U.U.A. continue
to fund Liberal Religious Youth in full, and hire a half-time staff
person as a consultant on youth programming to supplement their work.
A minority of the committee members endorsed an alternative recommendation

drafted by the committee's chair, the Rev. Bruce Southworth, suggesting
that the U.U.A. hire a full-time consultant on youth programs and not
continue to fund a full-time L.R.Y. staff of high-school-age people in
Boston.

The board of the U.U.A. rejected the majority report of the Y.A.C.
and endorsed instead the minority position, setting the scene for a floor
fight on the issue at the 1979 General Assembly in East Lansing, Michigan.

Following the death of U.U.A. President Paul Carnes, the Rev. O.
Eugene Pickett had been elected President of the association. Although
committed to a new full-time staff person in youth programs, he was open
to a compromise that would allow the L.R.Y. leadership to continue
working full-time as well. An ammendment to the Youth Caucus resolution
proposed by the Rev. Wayne Arnason and adopted by the General Assembly
opened the way for President Pickett and the leadership of L.R.Y. to
negotiate a compromise that would allow both staffing options to continue.
In September 1979, Pickett announced that Wayne Arnason would become the
first adult to work full-time in the area of U-U youth programming in
ten years.

Paths in the Jungle

It is difficult to make predictions about the future of the liberal
religious movement. It has continued to exist as a movement because it
remained rooted in local groups attached to Unitarian and Universalist
churches. These local group and federation structures are stubborn
organisms. They have faded out of existence in some areas, but can be
revived because a new group of people needs a youth program.

The significance of the continental level of L.R.Y. in the survival
and strength of the movement is a moot question. There has been a rela-

tively strong continental bureaucracy within the movement since the
re-organization of 1941, and it has made a tremendous difference in the
way L.R.Y. has seen itself, including the way local L.R.Y.'ers have seen
themselves.

They may never get involved beyond the local level, but they know
that they are part of a network of groups where others like themselves
are finding the same kind of friendship and nourishment. In whatever
form, I believe that a youth program with a continental structure and
a significant commitment to youth leadership and empowerment is important.

L.R.Y. and all its ancestors, A.U.Y., U.Y.F., Y.P.R.U., and Y.P.C.U.
have been a manisfestation of the irresistable need of young people to
share, to grow, to expand their awareness and their skills. The continued
support by the adult church of an essentially self-determining continental
youth program has added a unique dimension to the experience its participants have had over the years. Structures, styles of leadership, and
relationships with advisors and staff have changed to suit the needs of
the times, and they will continue to do so. Such changes have not and
need not in the future threaten the integrity of the educational philosophy underlying our youth programs. One shortcoming of an institutional
history such as this one is that it conveys only by inference the process
of religious education which underlies the experience that young persons
have within our movement.

I have appreciated the reflections of Hugo Holleroth concerning
the philosophy of religious education undergirding the curriculum series
of the Unitarian Universalist Association. Holleroth's reflections begin
with the assertion that we live in a world which is filled with power.
He summarized the objectives of Unitarian Universalist religious education

as follows:

> The overall objective of Unitarian Universalist religious
> education is to help children have a vivid and compelling
> experience of the Unitarian Universalist religion to help
> them achieve an orientation to the world. More specific
> objectives include helping them:
>
> – become aware of and comprehend the multitude of powers
> within the self as well as those which impinge upon
> them from the environing world;
>
> – discover and become skilled in using the process which is
> the Unitarian Universalist religion, and,
>
> – use the process which is the Unitarian Universalist
> religion for relating to and dealing with the ways they
> are affected by the world as intellectual, moral, sentient,
> aesthetic, and mortal beings.[2]

Adolescence is one of the periods in life when persons become acutely
aware of the powers that impinge upon them from within (such as their
own sexuality), as well as the powers that impinge upon them from without
(such as unjustified institutional restrictions). Furthermore, adolescence
is the first period in life when individuals can be given or can find
within themselves the personal power to actively respond to these power-
filled situations.

I see the liberal religious youth movements as an educational process
consistent with the Unitarian Universalist approach to religious education.
They have offered young people the opportunity to explore for themselves
the dynamic between freedom and responsibility in personal and institutional life in a world which is power-filled. Freedom and responsibility

cannot be understood as abstractions. They can only be grasped in living situations where real freedom and its consequential responsibility are present. This is the primary educational process that is going on within the chaos of local group meetings, federation conferences, and continental board meetings.

Another unique aspect of the educational process of our youth movement is the exposure it offers to the problems of life in groups and institutions. The themes of personal liberty vs. collective discipline, principles and ideals vs. institutional necessities, and individuality vs. group identity are consistently part of the experience of young people within our youth movement.

This is true on all levels of the organization, but particularly in regard to the continental level. The fact that an institutional history such as this one could be justified and compiled with a denomination of our size is testimony in itself to the influence our youth organizations have had on their members.

The only thing I am sure of about Unitarian Universalist youth is that they will continually re-invent the wheel. Advisors know the pattern well. It is one of the most frustrating things for people who have related to our youth movements over a long period of time. Similar problems and similar solutions occur and reoccur. Progress happens in a spiral, however. There are new environments that surround the old problems, and the old solutions are never quite the same as those of last year. It's a marvellous dance to watch. Reinventing the wheel is one of those things a liberal religious youth group is there for. There are no wisdom books or manuals to get people through adolescence into adulthood. It all reminds me of the image of the jungle in Gabriel Garcia

Marquez' book <u>One Hundred Years of Solitude</u>. One person hacks a path through it, but the jungle grows back as thickly as before as soon as the passage has been made. All that is left are stories of how the trail was made, but no markers to show you where it lies.

APPENDIX 1: YOUTH MOVEMENT PRESIDENTS

Y.P.R.U.		Y.P.C.U.	
		1889–92	Lee E. Joslyn
		1892–94	Herbert Briggs
1896–98	Thomas Van Ness	1894–97	Elmer Felt
1898–99	Roland W. Boynton	1897–1900	Harry M. Fowler
1899–1900	Walter Prichard Eaton		
1900–01	Roger S. Forbes	1900–05	Louis Annin Ames
1901–02	Percy A. Atherton		
1901–03	John Haynes Holmes		
1903 (5–11)	Edward Marsh		
1903(11)–04(5)	Earl C. Davis		
1904–05	Carleton Ames Wheeler		
1905–06	Edgar S. Wiers	1905–07	Frederick W. Perkins
1906–08	Harold G. Arnold		
1908–11	Henry G. Saunderson	1907–10	Harry R. Childs
1911–13	Dudley H. Ferrell	1910–12	A. Ingham Bushnell
1913–16	Sanford Bates	1912–15	Stanley Manning
1916–18	Frederick M. Eliot	1915–17	George A. Gay
		1917–18	Hal Kearns
1918–19	Carl B. Wetherell	1918–19	Eleanor Bisbee
1919–21	Houghton Page	1919–20	Samuel Cushing
		1920–21	Clifford Stetson
1921–22	Chester Allen	1921–22	Charles Taylor
1922–24	Albert A. Pollard	1922–23	Ernest Jones
1924–26	Edward P. Furber	1923–26	Ellsworth Reamon

Appendix 1, cont'd.

1926-28	Charles S. Bolster	1926-28	Carl Olson
1928-31	Frank B. Frederick	1928-29	Carl Olson
		1929-30	Dorothy Tilden Spoerl
1931-33	Dana McLean Greeley	1930-32	Max A. Kapp
1933-35	Bradford E. Gale	1932-34	Stanley Rawson
1935-38	John W. Brigham	1934-36	Arthur Olson
1938-39	Roland B. Greeley	1936-39	Benjamin Hersey
1939-41	Henry V. Atherton	1939-41	Fenwick.Leavitt

A.U.Y.   U.Y.F.

1941-43	G. Richard Kuch	1941-43	Dana Klotzle
1943-45	Arnold F. Westwood	1943-45	Ann Postma
1945-47	Elizabeth Green	1945-46	David Cole
1947-48	David B. Parke	1946-48	Robert H. Macpherson
1948-49	Kurt Hanslowe	1948-49	Carl Seaburg
1949-50	Charles W. Eddis	1949-51	Charles Collier
1950-52	C. Leon Hopper	1951-54	Rozelle Royall
1952-53	Eileen Layton		
1953-54	Clara Mayo		

L.R.Y.

1954-55	Clara Mayo
1955-57	Robert Johnson
1957-58	Richard Teare
1958-59	Spencer Lavan
1959-61	Jerry Lewis

Appendix 1, con'd

1961-62	Mary Vann Wilkins
1962-63	Maria Fleming
1963-64	Charles A. Forrester
1964-65	Frederick West
1965-66	William G. Sinkford
1966-67	Ruth Wahtera
1967-68	Gregory H. Sweigert
1968-69	Lawrence R. Ladd
1969-70	Robert L. Isaacs
1970-71	Lawrence Brown
1971-72	Charles B. Rosene
1972-73	Gale Pingel
1973-74	Adam Auster, Peter Nalven, (Office of President abolished) Paula Rose, Matthew Easton
1974-75	Lara Stahl, Bev Treumann, Steven Wilcox, David Knight
1975-76	Carlotta Woolcock, Lynn Rubinstein, Jennifer Shaw, Richard Taeuber, Gary Decker
1976-77	Emilie Blattman, Andrew Hanson, Paul Pigman, Doug Webb
1977-78	Abbe Bjorkland, Susan Buis, Shelley Cantril, Barbara Dykes
1978-79	Shelley Cantril, Katrinca Ford, Denise Lewis, Nada Velimirovic
1979-80	Cheryl Markhoff, Laurel Prager, Dave Williams, Gretchen Jones, Nina Martin, Julie Farman

APPENDIX 2: PRESIDENTS OF INTERNATIONAL RELIGIOUS FELLOWSHIP

1923   The Leyden International Bureau is founded with a secretariat
           in Holland.

1934   The L.I.B. is reorganized into International Religious
           Fellowship at a conference in Copenhagen, Denmark, and a
           formal Executive Committee is set up.

1934-38   Stewart Carter (Great Britain)

1938-39   Jeffrey Campbell (U.S.A.)

           World War II *see note 10 p.74

1947-48   G. Richard Kuch (U.S.A.)

1948-49   Ludek Benes (Czechoslovakia)

1949-50   Gerard Spelberg (Netherlands)

1950-52   Ronald McGraw (Great Britain)

1952-54   Kurt Jenney (Switzerland)

1954-56   Carel Delbeek (Netherlands)

1956-58   Axel Hoffer (U.S.A.)

1958-59   Donald Dunkley (Great Britain)

1959-61   Grenville Needham (Great Britain)

1961-62   Spencer Lavan (U.S.A.)

1962-64   Banz Probst (Switzerland)

1964-65   Martin Fieldhouse (Great Britain)

1965-67   Helmut Manteuffel (F.R. Germany)

1967-69   Andrew Patrick (Great Britain)

1969-71   Paul Reiber (U.S.A.)

1971-73   Geoff Blanc (France)

1973-75   Lucie·Meijer (Netherlands)

1975-76   Wayne Arnason (Canada)

Appendix 2, cont'd.

1976-78   Christine Hayhurst (Great Britain)

1978-80   Renate Bauer (F.R. Germany)

(This list was compiled by Helmut Manteuffel on the occasion
of I.R.F.'s 50th Anniversary in 1973)

FOOTNOTES

Notes to Introduction

1. This is not an unfamiliar complaint within the adult church as
    well.   There is always a gap between local expectations and
    denominational performance.

2. See Murdock, An Institutional History of the American Unitarian
    Association (U.U.A. Boston, 1975) for an excellent thesis on this
    lack of commitment.

3. The Universalist Leader, Vol. XXVII, No. 2. (Boston: Universalist
    Publishing House: January 12, 1924).

4. Quoted in Peter Baldwin, Ministry to Youth (Boston: Unitarian
    Universalist Association: 1964) P.18.

Chapter 1 Notes

1. C.H. Lyttle, Freedom Moves West (Boston: Beacon Press: 1952) p.230.

2. President William Howard Taft became active in the Unity Club in his
    home church in Cincinnati, Ohio, after graduating from Yale.   He later
    recalled that his presidential ambitions began with his election to
    the presidency of the Cincinnati Unity Club.

3. I notice as of the 1975 U.U.A. Directory that the Bay City, Michigan
    church has been dissolved.

4. Carl Henry and Herbert Briggs (ed.), "A Historical Souvenir of the
    Y.P.C.U." (1893).   Brochure located in the Universalist Historical
    Library at the Andover Harvard Library, Cambridge, Massachusetts
    (hereinafter referred to as U.H.L.).

5. Personal correspondence from Kelley to W. Gardner, Sept. 10, 1937.
    (U.H.L.)

6. I am indebted here to research done by Christopher Gist Raible at
    Starr King School, 1956-57, and to Arnold Crompton's Unitarianism
    on the Pacific Coast (Boston: Beacon Press: 1957).

7. Van Ness had been the A.U.A.'s Pacific Coast Mission Secretary from
    1889-1893, and was at that time minister of the Second Church in
    Boston.   He had the opportunity to see the different young people's
    groups on both coasts.

8. Crompton, op.cit., p. 158.

9. Nash became Dean of Lombard College. Shinn was the most celebrated of the Universalist missionaries. He was responsible for the creation of many churches. Ferry Beach was founded in 1901 out of the regular summer meetings Shinn conducted at The Weirs, New Hampshire, and later at Saco, Maine.

10. Henry and Briggs (ed.), op. cit., p. 11-12.

11. Quoted in Harry Adams Hersey, "A Brief History of the Y.P.C.U." in The Christian Leader, July 8, 1939 (Boston: Universalist Publishing House).

12. The church had a memorial stained glass window to Nash as well.

13. Harry Adams Hersey, op. cit., p. 637.

14. Quoted in F.B. Morris, "The Young People's Christian Union of Massachusetts and Rhode Island: A Complete History 1889-1939", p.7 (U.H.L.)

15. The provision for life membership remained in the Y.P.R.U., A.U.Y., and L.R.Y. constitutions, however. The most recent life memberships to be awarded were honorary ones given as tokens of esteem to Peter Baldwin upon his resignation as L.R.Y. Executive Director in 1966, to Dana Greeley, upon his retirement from the U.U.A. presidency in 1969, and to Carl Seaburg in 1978, for being a friend to many L.R.Y. Executive Committees.

16. Clinton Lee Scott, The Universalist Church of America: A Short History (Boston: Universalist Historical Society: 1957) p. 69.

17. F.B. Morris, op.cit., p. 12.

18. Harry Adams Hersey, op. cit., p. 697.

19. This menu is located in the Y.P.C.U. files, U.H.L.

20. From the minutes of the 1912 Y.P.C.U. Annual Meeting U.H.L.

Chapter 2 Notes

1. The Unitarians did not elect a woman as President until 1945.

2. Somewhat more than half of these actually affiliated and paid dues to the Y.P.R.U., however.

3. Raible would later enter the ministry with a long and distinguished career adminating in his ministry to the Unitarian Church in Dallas, Texas.

4. They were presidents 1926-28, and 1924-26 respectivively.

5. Robert Raible, in personal correspondence to Christopher Raible, 1956.

6. Harry Adams Hersey, op. cit., p. 646.

7. The Unitarian Church of Rowe received one share of Boston and Maine Railroad stock valued at $100,000.

8. Personal interview with Dana Greeley, January 28, 1976.

9. Harry Adams Hersey, op. cit., p. 650.

10. Again, I am indebted to Christopher Raible for access to personal correspondence from his father, Robert Raible, concerning his experiences in S.F.R.L.

Chapter 3 Notes

1. Personal interview with Dana Greeley, January 28, 1976.

2. Report of the Y.P.R.U. Committee on Interdenominational Relations, 1933. From the Y.P.R.U. files, Unitarian Universalist Association archives.

3. Clinton Lee Scott, op. cit., p. 70.

4. From the Y.P.R.U. files on the Peace Caravans. (U.H.L.)

5. Thanks to Gene Navias for telling us that "Follow the Gleam" was not Universalist in origin. The song is copyrighted by the Young Women's Christian Association of America, and was the Silver Bay Contest winner song at Bryn Mawr College.

6. The words to the Y.P.R.U. hymn were written by Sara Cumins, the Executive Secretary of the Y.P.R.U. during the mid 1920's.

7. These topics were chosen from a Y.P.C.U. group's program notes not only for their examplary nature but for the titles themselves as well.

8. From the Report of the 45th Annual Y.P.C.U. Meetings, October 12-14, 1934, p. 83. (U.H.L.)

9. Quoted in Benjamin Zablocki, The Joyful Community (Baltimore: Penguin Books: 1971), p. 66-67.

10. For these and other facts related to the early history of the free religious youth groups of Germany I am indebted to research undertaken by Deither Gehrmann printed as a monograph for the information of I.R.F. members in 1953.

Chapter 4 Notes

1. For a complete summary of the content and consequences of the
   Commission of Appraisal report, see the essay by Carol R. Morris,
   "It was Noontime Here" in C.C. Wright (ed.), A Stream of Light
   (Boston: Unitarian Universalist Association: 1975).

2. From Stepehn Fritchman's report accompanying the Senexet Re-
   organization Plan, April 16, 1942. p. 27.

3. Klotzle went on into the parish ministry and was the Unitarian
   Universalist Association's representative at the United Nations
   at the time of his death in 1974.

4. Raymond Hopkins became first Vice-President of the Unitarian
   Universalist Association.

5. From a 1949 report of the U.Y.F.'s Committee on Re-organization,
   Charles Harding, Chairman.

Chapter 5 Notes

1. See Ralph Lord Roy, Communism and the Churches (New York:
   Harcourt and Brace: 1960).

2. This incident is drawn from research by the Reverend Philip
   Zwerling for his unpublished manuscript, The Fritchman Case (1974).

3. Ibid.

4. Ibid.

5. Quoted in Ralph Lord Roy, op. cit., p. 466.

6. Letter to Phillip Zwerling, December 31, 1973.

7. Zwerling, op. cit. and The Christian Register various issues,
   1945-47. Valuable personal accounts of these years and events
   are found in S. Fritchman, Heretic (Skinner House: Boston 1977)
   p. 47-101.

8. From a copy of the telegram, dated May 27, 1947, in the private
   papers of David Parke.

9. This was unfortunately not to be. When the Iron Curtain fell
   shortly afterwards, Czechoslovakia was on the Communist side,
   and contact with the Czech groups became increasingly difficult.

10. I note that in compiling his list of I.R.F. Presidents and Conferences
    (see Appendix 2), Helmut Manteuffel did not consider the 1946 and

and 1947 I.R.F. gatherings to be official conferences, and does not list Karel Haspel in his list of Presidents. I assume that this is because the institutional structure of the post-war I.R.F. was not firmly established until after 1947.

11. Minutes of 1948 U.Y.F. Annual Meeting, Norway, Maine. (U.H.L.).

Chapter 6 Notes

1. Unitarian Unite! Report of the Commission on Planning and Review: October 15, 1947.

2. From dictated comments by Richard Kuch, January, 1975.

3. Conversation with David Parke, January 29, 1976.

4. The Christian Register, Vol. 129, No. 2 (February 1950).

5. Vol. 5, No. 4 (January, 1950).

6. From a personal interview with Alice Harrison; October, 1976.

7. Ibid.

8. The 1948 A.U.Y. Convention was held at Lake Couchiching, Ontario, Canada. Eddis was a Canadian, and at this conference held on Canadian soil, it was finally formally acknowledged that the A.U.Y. would be referred to as a "continental" rather than a "national" organization.

9. In this regard, we note a resolution passed by the A.U.Y. Council at its 1952 meetings, entitled "Repeal of Terrestial Law": "Moved: (L. Hopper) Whereas it is clearly evident that a 24 hour day is not sufficient to conduct our business, therefore be it resolved, that at following conventions A.U.Y. operate on a 40 hour day. Duly seconded and passed with Rising Acclamation."

10. Eileen Layton was the A.U.Y. President for 1952-53, and functioned virtually as Associate Director during that time. A.U.Y. hired her officially in mid-1952.

11. Leon Hopper: "A Short Subjective History of the Unitarian and Universalist Youth Movements" (A.U.Y. Files: 1963), p. 4.

Chapter 7 Notes

1. Kurt Jenny was the President of that Executive Committee, and Christopher Raible served as Corresponding Secretary.

2. From an interview with Alice Harrison, October 7, 1975.

209

3. Ibid.

4. L.R.Y.'s 1956 Annual Meeting minutes. U.U.A. Archives, Boston.

5. From Bill Gold's final report as Executive Director, 1956. U.U.A. Archives, Boston.

6. From Bill Gold's "Some observations on the basis of fifteen months as Executive Director of L.R.Y." U.U.A. Archives, Boston.

7. From Hopper's first report to the L.R.Y. Council, December, 1957, p. 3. (From Hopper's personal files.)

8. Lavan went on to become I.R.F. President as well.

9. The youth program conducted by the Church of the Larger Fellowship should be noted at this point. C.L.F. was founded in 1951 to provide services to isolated religious liberals. By the 1960's they published religious education material for their Junior Fellowship (age 6-11), Uniteens (age 12-14), Junior Fellowship Youth (J.F.Y. - age 15-18) and the Young Adults (age 18 - college age). J.F.Y. and the Young Adults affiliated with L.R.Y. and the Channing-Murray program, but by 1968 L.R.Y. had lost touch with them.

Chapter 8 Notes

1. Cf. The quote from Maria Fleming, pp. 4-5.

2. Fritz West, from "L.R.Y.: Fact and Vision", a 1966 L.R.Y. pamphlet. L.R.Y. files, 25 Beacon Street, Boston.

3. Friedman became a well-known concept artist.

4. U.U.A. President Dana McLean Greeley, and B.A.C. Chairman Hayward Henry.

Chapter 9 Notes

1. Fund-raising campaigns for the college in Europe and America were not successful, and it closed shortly after the move to Lausanne.

2. Hugo Holleroth, Relating To Our World (Boston: Beacon Press: 1974), p. 38.

INDEX